C000262922

The Great Train Robbery and the Metropolitan Police Flying Squad

THE GREAT TRAIN ROBBERY AND THE METROPOLITAN POLICE FLYING SQUAD

GEOFF PLATT

PEN & SWORD
TRUE CRIME

First published in Great Britain in 2015 by
Pen & Sword True Crime
an imprint of
Pen & Sword Books Ltd
47 Church Street
Barnsley
South Yorkshire
S70 2AS

ISBN 978 1 47382 380 8

A CIP catalogue record for this book is available
from the British Library

Typeset in Plantin by
Mac Style Ltd, Bridlington, East Yorkshire
Printed and bound in the UK by CPI Group (UK)
Ltd, Croydon, CR0 4YY

Pen & Sword Books Ltd incorporates the imprints
of Pen & Sword Archaeology, Atlas, Aviation,
Battleground, Discovery, Family History, History,
Maritime, Military, Naval, Politics, Railways, Select,
Transport, True Crime, and Fiction, Frontline
Books, Leo Cooper, Praetorian Press, Seaforth
Publishing and Wharncliffe.

For a complete list of Pen & Sword titles please
contact
PEN & SWORD BOOKS LIMITED
47 Church Street, Barnsley, South Yorkshire, S70
2AS, England
E-mail: enquiries@pen-and-sword.co.uk
Website: www.pen-and-sword.co.uk

Contents

Acknowledgements

A book, even a small paperback, is the culmination of a great deal of work over a long period of time and such a project requires that the author receives a considerable amount of support and understanding from his or her friends and colleagues.

It was whilst watching the Great Train Robbery on television on the BBC on 18 and 19 December 2013 that the idea of a book focusing on the 'other side' first occurred to me. So many books, films and television programmes had been written about the 'bad guys', 'the losers', the robbers who had been sentenced to up to thirty years imprisonment, yet almost nothing had been written about 'the good guys' 'the winners', the Police.

I mentioned this idea to my friend, the successful author, Dick Kirby, and encouraged him to take on the project. He cited personal reasons for not wanting to do so, but encouraged me to give it a try and referred me to his publisher, Pen and Sword and their Marketing Manager, Mr Jonathan Wright. He readily agreed a deal and sent me a contract to sign.

It was then, of course, that the full weight of the work that I had taken on, hit me!

I would like to express my appreciation to:

Thames Valley Police, their Chief Constable, Ms Sara Thornton CBE QPM, and the Curator of their museum, Mr Colin Boyes for their support and assistance as well as for allowing me to reproduce the statements made by their officers for the 50th Anniversary of the Robbery.

The Society of ex-CID officers of the Metropolitan Police, and their Secretary Bob Fenton QGM for his assistance in identifying and tracing officers on the enquiry.

The National Association for Retired Police Officers (NARPO), Judy Redford, the London Branch Manager and Julia Mullan, their IT Manager, for their assistance in identifying and tracing officers on the enquiry.

Geoff Platt

Preface

As the author has mentioned in the 'Acknowledgements' section of this book, he initially asked if I would wish to write an account of the Great Train Robbery. I demurred because (a) I was already heavily involved in writing another book, (b) I had already devoted a chapter to the Great Train Robbery in my history of the Flying Squad, *The Sweeney* and (c) I believed that – especially in the year of the 50th anniversary of the crime – quite enough books had been written on that particular subject. But with regards to (c), it just shows you how wrong one can be …

In this fascinating account of what the media referred to as 'The Crime of the Century', Geoff Platt has dug deep in his research to provide the reader with a gripping narrative of the planning of the heist and who did what, and why, from both sides of the fence – the cops and the robbers.

There are biographical accounts of the police officers involved in the investigation and the author describes precisely why they were the men best suited for the job of catching the men responsible for England's most audacious crime of the twentieth century. He has also cleverly introduced the points of view of some of the police officers from the Buckinghamshire Constabulary who contributed to the enquiry. Each of the arrested robbers also receives a biographical note and more importantly, we learn what happened to them after the trial.

There are insights into aspects of the investigation which have not previously been revealed and in a particularly even-handed fashion, Geoff Platt details mistakes made by all of the participants. The police – the calamitous decision by senior officers to publish details of the wanted men and their wives in the media; and the initial mistake in permitting the railway engine to be taken from the scene and thoroughly contaminated before an in-depth scientific forensic examination could be made. The robbers were at fault for failing to ensure that their hideout was not burnt to the ground; and the Post Office displayed staggering complacency for not providing adequate security for such an enormous sum of money.

Most interesting of all, Geoff Platt compares the investigation of the Great Train Robbery with other modern day major crime enquiries – how it was tackled then, and how it would be dealt with now. Would the Train Gang have been caught using today's methods? Then, information was recorded using 'The Scotland Yard System' – filing cards which were cross-referenced; now, records are computerised – but both systems are only as good as the people responsible for feeding in the information. Crime scene investigation has improved out of all recognition from half-a-century ago; detectives, too have changed. Would today's investigators have the contacts, the skills, the sheer cunning of their Flying Squad contemporaries of yesteryear to combat the top echelon of criminals?

This book provides at least some of the answers – and from the mass of information contained in its exciting and well put together pages, the readers can reach their own conclusions.

Dick Kirby
Former Flying Squad Detective.

Introduction

The Great Train Robbery occurred on 8 August 1963 and immediately caught the public's imagination as an audacious challenge to authority, represented by the Government, the Bank of England, the Post Office, British Rail and the Police. This was the post-Second World War period during which all authority was routinely challenged, the sexual revolution occurred and in which first 'Rock'n'Roll' and then 'Pop' music became popular. Public interest in the crime was extremely high and the Robbery dominated newspaper headlines for a fortnight.

An unprecedented series of newspaper articles, books, television shows and films have maintained an almost constant interest in the crime in the intervening period. The public have shown an insatiable appetite for stories about the criminals, their lives, what motivated them to do what they did, and the ways in which the Robbery changed their lives. Ronnie Biggs, who failed to perform his role in the Robbery satisfactorily, gained a reputation as a 'cheeky chappy' as he escaped from Wandsworth Prison and travelled across the world, thumbing his nose at authority and sending what appeared to be almost daily reports on his progress to the press. Despite running out of his share of the proceeds of the Robbery by 1966, he managed to generate a satisfactory income by giving press interviews, consulting on television programmes and films based on the Robbery, and making even more money than Tony Blair for posing for photographs, so as to be able to live comfortably for another thirty-five years.

As a 7-year-old boy, on 14 January 1963, I was taken by my parents to see the final journey of the Flying Scotsman, the train that made daily trips from London to Edinburgh. Then, in the summer of 1963, my family took in a businessman as a lodger and he frequently needed to send urgent letters to Scotland and my mother would take me up to Euston Station to deliver these letters to the travelling post office on the night train to Glasgow. When I heard about the Great Train Robbery in August 1963, it brought back memories of these trips and caught my imagination.

Since the time of the Robbery, I have lived on the border between Purley and Croydon, south of London. I remember regularly seeing Roy James shopping in our local shops in Purley, or driving his favourite Jaguar cars through Purley town centre. I would frequently see Bruce Reynolds walking past East Croydon Railway Station with his wife on his arm. If I caught the train to London, I would get off at Waterloo Station, to find Buster Edwards selling flowers from his stall outside the station.

When I grew up and became a Police Officer myself I started to meet other characters on the periphery of the crime, Freddie Foreman, Charlie Richardson and 'Mad' Frankie Fraser, as well as many of the detectives who had worked on the case. I also started to read the numerous books on the subject.

As a police officer I have been involved, among other cases, with the Brink's-MAT and the Knightsbridge Safe Deposit Centre robberies.

The Brink's-MAT robbery occurred early on 26 November 1983 when six robbers broke into the Brink's-MAT warehouse at Heathrow Airport, London. They stole £26 million (£75 million in today's money) worth of gold, diamonds and cash. They poured petrol over the staff and threatened to ignite it if they did not reveal the combination to the vault. The leader of the gang was one Mickey McAvoy and I was tasked with focusing on the McAvoy family business premises in Walworth. One day I arranged the simultaneous execution of twenty-six warrants on premises owned, occupied or controlled by the McAvoys. When the family's Rolls Royce was driven onto a ferry I arrested the driver, but 'forgot' to have the car returned to the dock. It remained in Portugal for twelve months! When McAvoy's brother drove the Rolls for a couple of weeks, without insurance, he complained to Scotland Yard when I arranged for him to receive eighty-one summonses for non-production of his driving documents (an average of six summonses a day!). More on the Brink's-MAT robbery later.

Valerio Viccei (1955–2000) was a prolific and very successful
armed robber, but due to the Italian criminal justice system, he
was never properly brought to justice. He arrived in London in
1986 when the Italian Police realised that he had become very
rich after committing over fifty armed robberies there. On 12
July 1987, two men entered the **Knightsbridge Safe Deposit
Centre** in Cheval Place, London SW7 and asked to rent a safe
deposit box. After being shown into the vault, they produced
hand guns, subdued the manager and security guards, and
left with an estimated £60 million, making it the third largest
robbery ever in the world. Of course, safety deposit boxes are
used by major criminals to hide their loot, so the sum taken
may have been ten times more than that which was admitted
by the owners. I was responsible for charging Viccei and the
manager of the Knightsbridge Safe Deposit Centre, Parvez
Latif, a cocaine user, who was heavily in debt, and who co-
operated in the robbery with Viccei. Viccei was sentenced to 22
years, serving his sentence in Parkhurst Prison on the Isle of
Wight. I felt some satisfaction as my family had built Parkhurst
in the 1790s. Unfortunately, in 1992, arrangements were made
for Viccei to serve the remainder of his sentence in Italy and
he was transferred to an open jail in Pescara, where he was
allowed to live a playboy lifestyle. On 19 April 2000, during a
day release from prison, a gunfight broke out between Viccei,
an accomplice, and the police, resulting in the death of Viccei.
Justice had, at last, been done.

It was whilst studying some of the books, television
programmes and films produced to mark the 50th Anniversary
of the Robbery, that it occurred to me that although the lives and
personalities of the robbers had been documented in detail, little
was generally known of the detectives from the Metropolitan
Police Flying Squad who had worked exceptionally hard and
exceptionally well for almost two years in order to bring the
Robbers to justice, and I started to believe that I was uniquely
qualified to produce a book on these officers who investigated
the Robbery, and on their investigation, its successes and its
failures. I was also aware that at the time of the Robbery, most
senior Scotland Yard detectives published an autobiography
as soon as they retired, but that the detective in charge of the

Robbery investigation, Detective Chief Superintendent Tommy Butler, extended his service so as to complete the enquiry and then died within months of retiring from the Metropolitan Police. I hope that this book will go some way to acknowledging his achievements and filling the void left by the absence of an autobiography.

It is now fifty years since the Robbery, and as all Police officers had to be at least twenty years of age before they could join the Service, even the youngest recruit must have now achieved his 'three score years and ten', with those who were experienced detectives at the time of the Robbery now nearer to 85 years of age. Unfortunately, only Detective Sergeant (later Detective Chief Superintendent) Stanley Moore from the initial squad is still alive, although Detective Inspector Peter Jones, who accompanied Detective Chief Superintendent Jack Slipper to Brazil to bring Ronnie Biggs back to England to complete his sentence, is also alive. I have enjoyed talking to both these men and found them both extremely interesting and intelligent and would like to express my appreciation for their co-operation in my book.

As a Police Officer, I am experienced in taking statements from witnesses, collating evidence and drawing out the essential facts from the rest of the clutter and explaining the significance of the facts for those not experienced in dealing with crimes such as armed robbery. I hope that I have used these skills well in the production of this book.

Ultimately, the reader will be the judge …

CHAPTER ONE

The Crime

(The story of the Great Train Robbery has been told many times over the last fifty years. This is simply a brief summary to place the rest of the book in context.)

In 1829, George Stephenson built *The Rocket* which was entered in, and won, the Rainhill Trials, by running up and down a mile-long length of track for longer than any of its four rivals. This success led to Stephenson establishing his company as the pre-eminent builder of steam locomotives used on railways in the UK, the US and much of Europe. It did not take long for the General Post Office (GPO) to recognise the value of railways to the service that they provided to the public, and in November 1830 the GPO agreed with the Liverpool and Manchester Railway for mail to be carried on the railway for the first time. Eight years later the Railways (Conveyance of Mail) Act was passed, which obliged railway companies to carry mail when required to do so by the Postmaster General, and trains carrying mail became known as Travelling Post Offices (TPOs).

These Travelling Post Offices experienced few problems with crime during the first one hundred and thirty years of their existence, but in the early 1960s there were a few thefts from the trains on the London to Brighton Line that prompted the GPO to review their security and design new secure carriages and improve security arrangements. These were about to be implemented when the Great Train Robbery occurred …

On Thursday 8 August 1963 at about 3.03 am the Royal Mail night train from Glasgow to London was stopped at Sears Crossing at Ledburn, near Mentmore in Buckinghamshire, by a gang of fifteen men, using a glove to cover the green signal and attaching a six-volt Ever Ready battery to illuminate the red signal.

The gang then mounted the engine, an English Electric Type 4 (later Class 40) diesel-electric locomotive number D326 (later 40 126) – curiously, the train had been involved in an accident that killed ten people a few weeks before the Robbery. They struck the train driver, Jack Mills over the head with a cosh, attacked his assistant, David Whitby, as he went to call the signal box for advice, and took control of the train.

They then detached the engine and the first two of the twelve carriages, containing parcels and High Value Packages (HVP) respectively, replaced Jack Mills with a retired train driver that they had recruited, and attempted to move the shortened train about half a mile to Bridego Railway Bridge (Bridge Number 127) now known as Mentmore Bridge.

The retired driver found that the train was different in design to the ones that he usually drove and that he could not release the brake, so the gang had to put Jack Mills back in control of the train and use threats of further violence in order to get him to move the train.

Moving the train to Bridego Bridge had the advantage of leaving behind seventy-two of the Post Office staff and a few British Rail employees on the train, who could have otherwise later been called upon to act as witnesses against the robbers should they later be arrested and put on trial. It also facilitated unloading the money from the train.

Bridego Bridge had been carefully selected by the gang due to its ideal location in a quiet area, relatively close to London, close to railway signals where the train could be stopped and easily accessible, by way of a short embankment, to main roads that facilitated a quick getaway. Here they forced entry to the HVP carriage and overcame the five staff working there, Thomas Kett, the Assistant Inspector in charge of the Post Office staff on the train, Frank Dewhurst the supervisor, and three other postal workers, Leslie Penn, Joseph Ware and John O'Connor, in order to rob them of 120 mailbags weighing about two and a half tonnes stuffed with £2,631,684.50 in used banknotes, mostly £1 and £5 notes (equal to about £45m in today's money, due to inflation), of which less than £400,000 has ever been recovered.

Following a security review in 1960, three of the HVP carriages had been equipped with bars over the windows, and bolts and catches on the doors and alarms, but on the day of the robbery these carriages were out of service, possibly due to sabotage, and a reserve carriage (M30204M) which had not been fitted with these security features had been taken into service. It had been proposed at the same time that the carriages should be fitted with radios in order to further improve security, but this was deemed to be too expensive and was not implemented.

Bruce Reynolds, the leader of the gang of robbers and the draughtsman for the job, allowed only thirty minutes to take the money and then instructed that the gang leave the train and jump into their transport to leave the scene and head for their 'slaughter' or hideaway. As the robbers decamped from the train, one of them made their first mistake by telling the Post Office staff not to move for thirty minutes, which caused the Police to believe that the robbers were hiding within thirty miles of the scene of the robbery.

The robbers had dressed themselves in military uniforms and disguised the Land Rovers and an Austin Loadstar lorry to look like military vehicles, due to the number of military camps in the area and the fact that this would allow them to move unnoticed and to exercise authority over anybody who hindered their escape. Between 3.45 am when they left the train and 4.30 am when they arrived at their getaway, they drove at high speed, through darkly-lit, winding, country lanes, until their reached the slaughter, just as the reports of the robbery reached the Police and radio messages started to be beamed across the county.

The robbers had cut all the telephone lines in the vicinity of the robbery, but one of the rail-men left on the train at Sear's Crossing caught a passing goods train to Cheddington, where he raised the alarm at around 4.20 am. The first reports of the robbery were broadcast on the VHF police radio within a few minutes and this is where the gang heard the line 'A robbery has been committed and you'll never believe it they've stolen the train!'

Leatherslade Farm is situated between Oakley and Brill in Buckinghamshire, approximately twenty-seven miles from Bridego Bridge. It was spotted by Bruce Reynolds and John Daly as they reconnoitred the area, mostly on a motorcycle, in the six months before the robbery and identified as a potential hideout. It had the benefit of being the only major farm in the area which did not appear on any local map. The farmhouse was later described as 'horrible, a mixture of everything – red brick, rendered, slates, felt, Roman tiles', but it was secluded and out of the way and with three bedrooms, two living rooms, a kitchen and a bathroom.

The gang tasked Brian Field, a solicitor's clerk who had previously worked on defending Gordon Goody, with arranging the purchase of the farm through his employer, John Wheater. Brian Field identified one of the firm's clients, Leonard Dennis Field (no relation) who had been granted power of attorney over his brother's affairs whilst the brother was serving a sentence of imprisonment and who was therefore in possession of spare cash, to assist him in the task. The two men visited the property and agreed to buy it by paying a 10% deposit in exchange for immediate access to the property in order, they claimed, to make improvements to the property, and then to pay the outstanding amount on completion of the purchase after the robbery, by which time they would have planned to have disappeared.

It was clear to the detectives who investigated the robbery, even after the crime, that the robbers had made a considerable effort to stock the farm for every eventuality. They had realised that twenty plus men may have had to stay there for up to ten, or even fourteen, days if things went badly and it appeared that the Police were close to catching them. All their needs had been carefully assessed and provided for.

Hatherill expressed the view that a woman had clearly been involved in selecting the food, drink and kitchen utensils that the robbers would need during their stay. And somebody had considered their warmth, comfort, sleep, transport and even entertainment needs. All this costs money and it is now recognised that the South West Gang had been retaining a percentage of the proceeds of their previous crimes in order to provide a float for the next job.

Living at the farm for a week would not have been easy. Space was restricted and this can bring about conflict, especially among large, aggressive men who are used to getting their own way. Stress about the Police getting closer and the risk of capture and punishment will also exacerbate the situation. There was plenty of food and drink and the robbers were keen to keep up with Police progress in the enquiry on the radio. There was ample space outside the farmhouse where those that wanted to could play sport or keep fit. Some of the robbers, obviously, kept themselves entertained counting out the money and sorting out the various shares and 'drinks' for the gang members.

Reynolds' plan involved the robbers keeping their heads down at the farm for seven days, as they relaxed after their exertions, counted their money, shared it out between them, and let the heat of the Police investigation blow over. They listened to Police broadcasts and BBC Radio news and it was in this way that they learned that the Police were planning to search every 'gas station, residence, warehouse, farmhouse, henhouse, outhouse and doghouse' within a thirty mile radius of the robbery.

Pressure then grew amongst the gang to leave the farm earlier than had been originally planned. They heard on the radio that military vehicles had been seen in the area at the time of the robbery and realised that they could no longer use the same vehicles when they left the farm. They undertook experiments in painting the vehicles with some bright yellow paint that they had found on the farm, but these were deemed a failure and it was eventually decided to send out a couple of robbers to collect other vehicles in which the gang would eventually withdraw from the farm, while the Austin Loadstar lorry and the Land Rovers were left at the farm. Yellow paint from the farm was later found on the property of two of the robbers and led to their conviction.

Reynolds's plan required all gang members to wear gloves at all times, but the robbers found it uncomfortable to wear gloves at night or when using the toilet, or to replace the gloves after sleeping or using the toilet, so fingerprints were left in the farmhouse. Reynolds told the gang to clean up the farmhouse before they left, and they complied, but these were not men experienced in housekeeping and they soon bored of it. But it didn't matter anyway, because they all knew that there was a 'Dustman' coming along to burn the place down after they left.

Except that when the gang made enquiries a few days later they found that the 'Dustman' had got cold feet and failed to clean up after them, or to burn the place down, despite accepting a 'drink' of £28,500. When he was told this, Goody wanted to kill Brian Field who had accepted responsibility for finding somebody to do the job when the original incumbent had been arrested before the robbery.

On Sunday night the gang drove out of the farm and up to London where they went their separate ways and the robbery plan effectively ended. The robbers had been told that there might be as much as £1 million on the train and they had been surprised to find £2.6 million. The robbers should have placed the money in safety deposit boxes and only later distributed it, so that nobody became suspicious at gang members suddenly becoming rich after the crime – but they did not.

Local residents later remembered that the robbers used to go to the Royal Oak pub in Oakley. 'They used to go in separately. They never spoke to each other and no one knew it was them until afterwards.'

CHAPTER TWO

The Conspiracy

(The essential element of the crime of Conspiracy is the agreement by two or more people to carry out a criminal act. Even if nothing is done in furtherance of the agreement, the offence of Conspiracy is complete)

All the principal participants in the Great Train Robbery were charged with Robbery and Conspiracy to Rob, so it is necessary to understand what conspiracy means and to review the details of the planning that the gang undertook before they committed the robbery.

Conspiracy to commit an indictable offence (a serious crime triable at the Assizes or Crown Court) was originally conceived by trial judges who recognised that there are occasions where a substantive offence may not have been completed but nevertheless an offence of a different kind has been committed because of the actions or agreements in preparation for the substantive offence; these are known as inchoate offences.

All crimes require a guilty mind (*mens rea*) and a guilty act (*actus reus*). For conspiracy the *actus reus* is the agreement. This cannot be a mere mental operation; it must involve spoken or written words or other overt acts. If the defendant repents and withdraws immediately after the agreement has been concluded, he or she is still guilty of the offence.

There must be an agreement to commit the criminal offence, but the motives of the conspirators are irrelevant. For example, it has been accepted by the courts that the fact that one conspirator was an undercover police officer (who only entered the conspiracy to catch drug dealers) did not prevent the offence of conspiracy from being committed.

As a boy, Bruce Reynolds was told by his father that it did not matter what he did in his life, but he must always try to be the best at it. This advice made a strong impression on Reynolds so that when he decided that he was going to make his living as a professional thief, he promptly decided that he wanted to be the best thief. He would frequently discuss his ambition with friends and colleagues and was constantly seeking ways to improve his skills and steal greater prizes.

The popular view, expressed in many books on the Robbery, is that at the end of 1962 Brian Field was sent to court to liaise between Gordon Goody's solicitor (Wheater) and barrister, in the trial for the Armed Robbery at the BOAC Offices at Heathrow Airport. At the end of the trial, Goody was acquitted and Field is alleged to have introduced him to 'The Ulsterman', a mysterious figure who is alleged to have worked for the Post Office and to have proposed the Great Train Robbery and provided much of the information necessary to make it happen. Goody is then believed to have sold the idea of the Robbery to Reynolds and the rest of the gang.

Detective Inspector Frank Williams who managed the Flying Squad team which investigated the Robbery, in his autobiographical book *No Fixed Address*, tells a very different story. As his boss, Detective Chief Superintendent Tommy Butler, Head of the Metropolitan Police Flying Squad and the man who led the team which investigated the Robbery, described him as the 'Best Informed Officer in the Metropolitan Police' maybe he did know best.

Williams' view was that in 1961, two years before the Robbery, Reynolds decided that robbing trains was the way forward and would provide the best profits. He then went around London meeting with all the leaders of the biggest and best criminal gangs seeking a partnership that would allow planning for the 'Crime of the Century' to proceed, but none of the other gangs were interested in Reynolds' idea. There were regular, frequent and easy pickings to be achieved from the common wage robberies and bank robberies, so why should they upset the equilibrium and get the Police and the Courts all fired up about a spectacular crime?

Eventually, Reynolds, the leader of a gang of robbers based in Walworth and Bermondsey, met up with Roger Cordrey, the leader of a gang of robbers based in Sutton and Wimbledon, and they agreed to form a partnership to work towards a major train robbery. As part of the plan, Reynolds' gang continued their regular work robbing banks and safe-blowing so as to generate income, with a healthy percentage being set aside to fund 'the big tickle' or 'the enterprise' as it became known. Cordrey took his gang down to Brighton and started to get to grips with the complexities of train robbery, such as the way to stop trains and the way to uncouple carriages, etc.

Police records show a series of six unsolved train robberies on the London to Brighton line during this period and it is very likely that Cordrey's gang committed all of these. Cordrey experimented with various ways to stop trains, ranging from pulling the communication cord on a train carrying passengers, through a range of other ideas, to the method that he eventually used in the Great Train Robbery, where he covered the green signals with gloves and used a six volt battery to illuminate each of the red signals. Bill Boal was tasked with experimenting with ways to uncouple carriages and soon became proficient in this.

Around January 1963 the leaders of the two gangs got together for a meeting, where it was decided that the preparations for the train robbery had been completed with Reynolds' gang, now known locally as the 'South West Gang' having raised the funds that would be required for such an operation, and Cordrey's gang, now known as the 'South Coast Raiders' for their success in robbing trains, having become skilful and experienced in stopping and uncoupling trains. They could now start to prepare for 'the enterprise'. An 'inside man', who worked for the Post Office and knew the workings of the Night Mail Train from Glasgow to London was signed up. Preliminary scouting missions of likely places where the Robbery could be committed were conducted on a motorcycle.

The leaders of the two gangs selected a group from among them to act as 'the committee' to undertake the research and planning necessary for such a considerable exercise. Bruce Reynolds appears to have chaired this committee, whose members were Gordon Goody, Charlie Wilson and Buster Edwards from the South West Gang and Roger Cordrey from the South Coast Raiders. A committee brings the benefits of many minds working together and increasing co-operation, but encourages doubt and delay at vital stages of the robbery. This is the way that it proved during the Great Train Robbery.

Soon it was decided by 'the committee' that the Robbery would have to take place between Rugby, where the train made its last cash pickup, and the London suburbs, where the Robbery might be overlooked from local houses and flats. Following weeks of extensive research it was decided that the perfect venue was near Cheddington in Buckinghamshire, where the train could be stopped at signals at Sears Crossing and, following the uncoupling of the engine and the target HVP carriage, the train could be driven to an embankment and lonely isolated road at Bridego Bridge.

There was a heated and protracted debate among 'the committee' about whether, after the robbery, they should make a dash for London or sit out the anticipated police activity in a hideout. Roy James and some of the others felt that they should make a dash for London using fast cars and relying on the excellent drivers available to them, but this would mean that the proceeds of the Robbery would have to be left to the gentle mercies of just a few gang members who could then cheat the rest of the gang out of their shares of the proceeds. So the only solution was for the money and the gang to stay together until it had been shared out. Clearly, a hideout would be required.

It was at this time that 'the committee' decided to seek legal advice on their plan and the ways in which they might take steps to reduce the likelihood of detection and the potential sentences meted out to any gang member who was caught by the police, and they approached a disbarred barrister. He advised that a crime such as was planned would provoke a national outcry and force a reaction from the government, so that any robbers arrested could expect a sentence of up to thirty years imprisonment. He suggested that the gang should agree three rules and require each gang member to accept them and agree to comply with them. These rules were:

1. No firearms;
2. No violence;
3. No talking to the Police.

'The Committee' required every candidate for the gang to take an oath to comply with these rules, and certainly no firearms were ever found or used on the Robbery. The only incidence of violence was the assault on the train driver, Jack Mills, from which he never recovered before his death seven years later. Various robbers have admitted responsibility for assaulting the train driver, but the consensus is that the assault was committed by one of three uncharged robbers, who were interviewed by the Police, but against whom insufficient evidence was ever found. Although no evidence was ever given in court of any robber talking to members of the Police, Frank Williams claims to have spoken to several of them and their representatives and friends about returning some of the proceeds of the Robbery.

'The committee' decided that they needed certain specialists to stop the train, to uncouple the carriages, to buy the hideout and to complete the conveyancing. They also decided that they needed more muscle, in order to intimidate the seventy-seven Post Office staff on the train and to assist in carrying the two and a half tons of mailbags out of the train, down the embankment and into the lorry. This is where Reynolds employed his knowledge of business practice and a selection process and a selection committee was arranged.

Applications were then invited for both the skilled and unskilled positions in the gang, although no man was allowed to apply until he had satisfactorily completed two other robberies under the watchful eye of two 'minders' appointed by 'the committee'. This would show whether he could follow instructions without question and whether he could be trusted to remain silent even in the face of harsh police questioning as might be expected after the crime of the century.

During July 1963 the gang moved into the final stages of their preparations for the robbery. Brian Field applied constant pressure to the Rixons, the family selling Leatherslade Farm, to concede to his client's request to move out of the farm so that he could arrange for the restoration work to be undertaken. The Rixons eventually moved out on 29 July, just nine days before the date fixed for the robbery, allowing the gang to take possession of the farm and make their final preparations.

As 'the committee' had decided that they wanted to appear to be Army units during the robbery, the simplest way to obtain their vehicles was from the War Department, who held frequent auctions to dispose of vehicles and equipment that they no

Name	Affiliation	Pre-robbery task	Task during the robbery
Bruce Reynolds	South West Gang	Draughtsman for the robbery	Leader of the gang
Gordon Goody	South West Gang	Member of 'the committee'	Heavy employed to intimidate and carry mail sacks
Charlie Wilson	South West Gang	Member of 'the committee'	Heavy employed to intimidate and carry mail sacks
Buster Edwards	South West Gang	Member of 'the committee'	Heavy employed to intimidate and carry mail sacks
Roy James	South West Gang	Responsible for specifying the vehicles required	Responsible for uncoupling HVP from train. Then used as getaway driver
John Daly	South West Gang	None	Responsible for assisting to 'fix' the train signals so as to stop the train
Roger Cordrey	South Coast Raiders	Member of 'the committee'	Responsible for 'fixing' the signals so as to stop the train
Bob Welch	South Coast Raiders	None	Heavy employed to intimidate and carry mail sacks
Jim Hussey	South Coast Raiders	None	Heavy employed to intimidate and carry mail sacks
Bill Boal	South Coast Raiders	None	Responsible for uncoupling HVP from train
Jimmy White	Lone Thief	Responsible for securing the vehicles	Heavy employed to intimidate, and to carry mail sacks. Then drove lorry carrying cash from scene to farm
Ronnie Biggs	Lone Thief	Responsible for finding train driver to assist during robbery	Responsible for 'minding' train driver during robbery.
John Wheater	Solicitor	Responsible for conveyancing the purchase of the farm	None

Name	Affiliation	Pre-robbery task	Task during the robbery
Brian Field	Solicitor's Clerk	Acted as the intermediary to bring the inside man together with the gang	None
Lennie Field	A merchant sailor of previous good character	Employed as the 'face' to buy the farm	None

longer required. An Austin goods platform truck was purchased by a dealer at an auction on 24 April and sold on to Jimmy White. A Land Rover index number BMG 757A was sold at another auction on 2 July to another dealer, who also sold it to Jimmy White. Three weeks later, on 21 July, White went out and stole another similar Land Rover from Oxenden Street, London WC2. He then took the vehicles away to be painted and stored until they were required for the robbery.

Jimmy White purchased the military uniforms and overalls required by the gang and arranged for Charlie Wilson to purchase all the food that the gang would require during their stay at the farm. Finally the gang members were told to make their way to the farm individually under their own steam by Wednesday 7 August 1963. Everything was now ready for the robbery to go ahead as planned.

Nowadays lawyers, accountants, academics and professionals are frequently found committing large-scale fraud, money laundering or even drug dealing, but armed robbery is usually committed by professional thieves with extensive lists of convictions, who spend substantial periods of time in prison, and therefore possess a poor employment history. The Great Train Robbery must have been one of the first crimes of this type in history to have taken legal advice during the planning process or to have used selection committees, formal references, probationary periods and oaths of obedience in the selection of the robbers.

Having prepared so comprehensively, they probably deserved a 'result'.

CHAPTER THREE

The Robbers

(Again, most people know the identity and biographies of the robbers – this chapter is a brief summary to refresh readers' memories)

The Robbers and their Friends

Men who received 'drinks'

Full Name	Role	Birth/death	Age on day
'Mark the Dustman'	Brian Field's pal who was responsible for cleaning up the farm and then burning it down	Never publicly identified	
'Stan (Pop) Agate'	Biggs' pal employed to replace the train driver		67
Leonard Denis Field	No relation to Brian Field. Employed to purchase farm	xx/xx/31	31
John Denby Wheater	Solicitor and employer of Brian Field. Carried out conveyance of Leatherslade Farm	17/12/21 to xx/7/85	41
William Gerald Boal	Friend of Roger Cordrey, the leader of the South Coast Raiders, with whom he was arrested. Believed to be responsible for discovering method of uncoupling train carriages. May or may not have been involved in the actual robbery.	22/10/13 to 26/6/70	49

Those who received a share of the proceeds

Full Name	Affiliation/Gang	Role	Born and died	Age on day	Arrested	Released
Bruce Richard Reynolds	South West	Leader	7/9/31 to 28/2/13	31	9/11/68	1978
Douglas (Gordon) Goody	South West	Deputy Leader	11/3/30 to present	33	3/10/63	1975
Charles Frederick Wilson	South West	Treasurer	30/6/32 to 23/4/90	31	22/8/63	1978
Ronald Christopher (Buster) Edwards	South West	Organiser	27/1/31 to 28/11/94	32	xx/9/66	1975
Roger John Cordrey	S. Coast Raiders	Train stopper	30/5/21 to xx/xx/05	42	13/8/63	1971
Robert Alfred Welch	S. Coast Raiders	Muscle	12/3/29 to present	34	25/10/63	1976
Thomas William Wisbey	S. Coast Raiders	Muscle	27/4/30 to present	33	11/9/63	1976
James (Big Jim) Hussey	S. Coast Raiders	Muscle	8/4/33 to 12/11/12	34	xx/xx/64	1975
Bill (Flossy) Jennings	S. Coast Raiders	Train uncoupler	Not disclosed	?	Not arrested	Not arrested
Frank Munroe	S. Coast Raiders	Muscle	Not disclosed	?	7/9/63	Not charged
Roy John (Weasel) James	Driver for hire	Getaway driver Train uncoupler	30/8/35 to 21/8/97	28	10/10/63	1975
John Thomas (Paddy) Daly	Reynolds' brother in law	Getaway driver Train stopper	6/6/31 to 10/4/13	32	3/12/63	Acquitted
James Edward White	Reynolds' pal	Quartermaster/ train uncoupler	21/2/20 to unknown	43	21/4/66	1975
Ronald Arthur Biggs	Reynolds' pal	Found and supported retired train driver	8/8/29 to 18/12/13	34	4/9/63	2009
Brian Arthur Field	Solicitor's clerk	Link to Ulsterman and bought L. Farm	15/12/34 to 27/4/79	28	15/9/63	1967
"Alf Thomas"	White's pal	Muscle	Never publicly identified, although interviewed by Police.			
"Ulsterman"	British Rail employee and instigator of robbery.		Never publicly identified.			

CHAPTER FOUR

The Police

(This is the first time that the personality and achievements of the officers who conducted the enquiry has been discussed. It's very interesting!)

The Men from Scotland Yard

Commander George Hatherill

George Hatherill was a unique Police Officer. He was a huge man, a highly-skilled linguist, held a rank equal to that of a current Deputy Assistant Commissioner and headed the Metropolitan Police Criminal Investigation Department for seven years, during which he doubled its size and totally reorganised it. But it is the fact that he spent only ten weeks wearing a uniform and walking a beat that makes him unique. Just about every other Police Officer in history has had to spend two years learning his job.

Hatherill was very well educated. He was fluent in six languages and skilled in shorthand. From an early age his enquiring mind had taken him all over London, all over Europe, and then all over the World.

He was born in Dulwich in South East London in July 1898. He attended a local primary school where he discovered an interest in languages, starting with French, so that by the age of 12 he was able to speak and write French and derived as much pleasure from reading books in French as from reading books in English. He also started to notice that he did not need to translate the books into English in order to understand them and was capable of thinking in French. It was at this time that he made the decision to see whether his skills allowed him to learn other languages, and he started learning German, then Polish.

Whilst at primary school, George would take himself to local museums, art galleries and libraries, where he could find a wide range of books on subjects that interested him, and he developed a lifelong interest in reading. It was whilst at the local Peckham Road Library that he met another young man, with whom he engaged in protracted and intense debates about life. Their conversations continued for over forty years, until Cecil Louis Troughton Smith had left Dulwich College, given up his medical studies at Guys Hospital, and written the Hornblower series of books under his pen name of C.S. Forester.

As he grew and his confidence developed, he started walking further and further in his quest to visit more museums, galleries and libraries. Then he found that using buses he could travel all over London and get to know the different races and cultures that lived there, a useful skill for an embryonic Police Officer.

When he was given a bicycle for his 13th birthday, he found that he could make it to Brighton and the south coast and made regular trips there. Aged 15 he made his first trip across the Channel, to France and later to Belgium. He found on the Continent more museums, art galleries and libraries to satisfy his enquiring mind.

Hatherill discovered shorthand when he was seventeen and decided that this would be a useful life skill. He taught himself, developing his skills by attending church on Sundays and transcribing the sermons that he heard. It took him almost a year of attending church to be able to keep up with the sermons and produce reliable and accurate records that satisfied him.

He first applied to join the Army before he was 18 years old, but despite his height of 6'6" and bulky frame he failed to deceive the selectors and was turned away. Eventually he met a soldier in the Queen Victoria's Rifles and, liking the fact that their uniform included black buttons that did not require constant cleaning as did the shiny metal ones that most other regiments wore, he went to the regimental headquarters in Davies Street in Mayfair, applied to join, and was accepted.

For the next three years he was employed as an interpreter, working on a wide range of political, intelligence and criminal matters, until it was time for him to return to England to be demobilised. Upon his return he wasted no time in finding work, starting the next day and working in the only clothes that fitted him, his army uniform. However, working in an office did not suit him at all and, in desperation, he approached a policeman in London to discuss his situation. He decided to join the Metropolitan Police.

After two months training, he was sworn in as a Police Officer in the Metropolitan Police on 2 February 1920. Ten weeks later, on uniformed patrol in St John's Wood, he saw an invitation in Police Orders for officers to apply for vacancies in Special Branch, the department responsible for investigating political crimes and protecting VIPs. The requirements included a knowledge of foreign languages and of shorthand.

Although the object of considerable ridicule from his senior officers for his audacity in applying for the post in Special Branch, the laugh was on them when George was selected and quickly inducted into the Branch as a Detective Constable.

After five years working on general Special Branch duties, Hatherill was given the choice of Paris or Brussels for a two year overseas posting, liaising with the local government on security and intelligence issues. He chose Brussels, but the posting lasted for seven years rather than two. He spent his holidays travelling around Europe, particularly Scandinavia.

When he eventually returned to England, Hatherill felt bored with Special Branch work and applied for a transfer to general CID duties. Knowing nothing about criminal investigation, he spent four months teaching himself criminal law, criminal court procedure and methods of criminal investigation. He was appointed to the CID in 1932.

In October 1938 Hatherill was promoted to Detective Chief Inspector and posted to the Murder Squad at Scotland Yard. But at the outbreak of the Second World War, the British Government became alarmed at the amount of property that was being stolen and sought advice from Scotland Yard as to the ways of dealing with this. Hatherill was sent to Europe to investigate and returned to submit proposals for a Special Investigations Branch (SIB) staffed by former Scotland Yard detectives.

In 1943, Hatherill was promoted to the rank of Superintendent and placed in command of the CID in East and North East

London. Three years later, he was transferred back to Scotland Yard to take charge of the CID officers posted there.

In 1951, seeing no further opportunities for advancement and seeking a role with shorter, less stressful, hours and less strenuous duties, he began to consider retirement as an option and to discuss this with his colleagues. To his surprise, he was offered the post of Deputy Commander in the Uniformed Branch, in which he had had only ten weeks experience, thirty-one years earlier.

In the interim, technology had changed policing considerably, with the introduction of cars, motorcycles, radios, and automatic alarms. He accepted the role and was posted as the Number 2 in charge of 1 District covering North West London from Westminster to Heathrow Airport and including responsibility for both Royalty and Government. He later admitted that he had spent his first three months studying the Instruction Book issued to junior officers to advise and instruct them in their work.

Almost as soon as he had settled into his new post, King George VI died and Hatherill was required to take command of his State Funeral and the Coronation of Queen Elizabeth II. Hatherill gained considerable knowledge and experience of uniformed duties over the next two years and had time to review the work of the CID and liaison between the uniform and CID.

After two years in uniformed duties, in 1957, Hatherill was summoned to meet the Commissioner who asked him to accept an appointment as Commander of the Criminal Investigation Department.

Hatherill accepted the offer and started a fundamental enlargement and restructuring of the CID. The number of detectives was doubled. Existing squads, such as the Flying Squad, Regional Crime Squad, and Fraud Squad were doubled in size, and new squads were established to deal with Stolen Vehicles, Criminal Intelligence etc., and the expansion and development of the Detective Training School.

In July 1963 Hatherill reached his statutory retirement age and met with the Commissioner, Sir Joseph Simpson. Sir Joseph proposed that after six years spent restructuring the CID he should delay his retirement in order to evaluate the results of his efforts. Hatherill accepted the offer and deferred his retirement for twelve months. Four weeks later the Great Train Robbery occurred and hopes of a gentle slowing and relaxation into retirement were lost forever.

On the morning of the Great Train Robbery, Hatherill arrived at Scotland Yard an hour before the first edition of the *Evening Standard*, London's evening newspaper, appeared on the streets. The paper gave a brief account of what had happened and assessed the loss at approximately £1 million. As he came to terms with the report, a telex arrived from the Chief Constable of Buckinghamshire, Brigadier John Cheney, setting out the facts.

Attempts were made to contact the Chief Constable, but all telephone lines were constantly engaged and no contact could be made. Nevertheless Hatherill called a meeting of the senior officers of the Flying Squad, the Regional Crime Squad and the Intelligence Squad, but without direct contact with Buckinghamshire Constabulary or specific information, little could be done.

As the meeting with the senior officers ended, Hatherill received a call from the Chief Constable. He set out the facts, requested Scotland Yard's assistance in the enquiry, and suggested a face-to-face meeting at a conference taking place that afternoon at the GPO with the Post Office Investigations Branch and the British Transport Police.

A review of resources revealed that the Assistant Commissioner (Crime), Sir Richard Jackson was at an Interpol Conference and Hatherill was covering his absence. Hatherill's two deputies were also absent, one at the Interpol Conference and one seriously ill in hospital. Five of the Detective Superintendents on the Murder Squad and three of the four Detective Superintendents on Area were engaged on provincial Murder enquiries. In addition to that, being August, many officers were on holiday.

Hatherill took Detective Superintendent Gerald McArthur, the officer that he had decided to send to assist Buckinghamshire Constabulary, with him to the GPO Conference and appointed Detective Chief Superintendent Millen and the Flying Squad to deal with the vast amount of information being received at Scotland Yard relating to the robbery.

As a result of the Great Train Robbery, the Metropolitan Police gave the Flying Squad unfettered freedom to seek out the robbers. Unlimited overtime was authorised and detectives were relieved of their routine responsibilities. The number of criminals being stopped and searched, the number of addresses searched and suspects arrested increased drastically. Statistically, this had the effect of creating a crime wave, with the number of crimes in London more than doubling. Eventually, so much information was being received about the robbery, and so much work being generated about other crimes, that half of the CID officers in London were engaged on these enquiries.

Two days later, as matters became clearer, Hatherill re-evaluated the situation and amended his postings. Detective Superintendent Gerald McArthur was tasked with collating and evaluating the substantial number of statements that were being gathered. Detective Superintendent Malcolm Fewtrell of Buckinghamshire Constabulary was made responsible for the charging of all prisoners and related correspondence. 'The Terrible Twins' of Detective Chief Superintendent Tommy Butler and Detective Chief Inspector Peter Vibart were brought in to assist Detective Chief Superintendent Ernie Millen with the main enquiry and the arrest of suspects. Later Tommy Butler would be instructed to take over the enquiry from Ernie Millen, who would be appointed Deputy Commander in charge of the CID.

Now Hatherill's responsibility was to monitor the work of his officers, give advice, and report to politicians and press as necessary. With his best officers deployed, there was not too much for him to do. By the time that he completed his extension of service, the enquiry was well established, suspects were being arrested, and he could rest happy that his job was done and he could retire from the Metropolitan Police.

Hatherill joined the Metropolitan Police in 1920 and retired in 1964 and therefore completed forty four years service, which must be close to a record. He joined at age 22, the requirement being that recruits must be at least 20, and he retired following an extension from the normal statutory retirement age of 65, at the age of 66.

By the time that he retired Hatherill had investigated fifty murders. Two thirds of these had resulted in convictions for Murder, and the rest in convictions for Manslaughter; six men had been hanged. Many of these crimes had been committed in the counties, outside the Metropolitan Police District, meaning that Hatherill had completed more than a third of his service in the Metropolitan Police outside the UK and more than a half of it outside the MPD.

Assistant Commander Ernie Millen

During the Robbery enquiry, DCS Ernie Millen was Deputy Commander in charge of the CID.

In his younger days he had the rare distinction of working with the renowned Home Office Pathologist, Sir Bernard Spilsbury on a murder investigation, before he had even considered a career in the Police. As an apprentice pharmacist for Boots the Chemist, at their Cliftonville branch, near Margate in Kent, Millen dispensed a prescription for a substance containing arsenic to a man called Sidney Fox. Fox had been accused of murdering his mother in room 66 of the Metropole Hotel in Margate by setting fire to the room. He, in turn, claimed that she had died due to an incorrectly-dispensed prescription. Millen was interviewed by the Police and made a statement, but then met with Spilsbury to answer some more specific questions. The jury convicted Fox and he was hanged at Maidstone Jail on 8 April 1930.

Born in Westgate-on-Sea near Margate in Kent in 1911, the son of a railway worker, and educated at the local Church of England Primary School, Millen had a long-held ambition to become a doctor, but his grades were not sufficient. His father was not in a position to provide the financial support for him to secure the grades that he required, and he hoped that his employment as an apprentice pharmacist would assist him in achieving his goal.

In 1934, responding to protracted pressure from his father to accept that he was not going to achieve his ambition of becoming a doctor, and returning from the West Country on a train, Millen read a newspaper advert seeking recruits to the Police. He realised that competition was fierce, but felt confident that his education, his height of six foot, and his sturdy physique from active participation in sports such as boxing and swimming would stand him in good stead. His confidence was justified. He joined the Metropolitan Police in 1934, just after his 23rd birthday and was posted to Gerald Road Police Station, now part of Belgravia Division.

Millen made a steady start to his career and after a period as an 'aid to CID' was selected to join as a Detective Constable at Arbour Square Police Station in the East End in January 1938. He was sent to live at the Section House at Violet Road in Bethnal Green, the only CID officer among sixty uniformed officers.

His first job in his new post was to investigate an allegation of 'Bestiality with a Horse' – and there are not many of those! Millen went to the office and read the book on what to do and came back to see the uniformed Inspector on duty, who, according to the regulations, was the only person authorised to accept a charge in such cases. Throughout his service, Millen relied on his education to explore the law and instigate unusual investigations that others may have allowed to slip past them.

Life in Bethnal Green must have come as a shock after life in Knightsbridge and the young Millen decided that he wanted to marry his fiancée and set up home with her. The problem with this was that Police Regulations did not permit officers with less than ten years service to marry or to live anywhere other than at a Section House. Despite the ban, Millen submitted a report to his Chief Superintendent, informing him that he wished to marry his fiancée, Ena, that she had her own income from her job as a school teacher, and that her 'condition made it urgently desirable we should marry.' Authority to marry and to move into Police Married Quarters was granted in double quick time, but Millen paid the price when his boss, Detective Superintendent Symes, presented Ena with a wedding present on behalf of Ernie's CID colleagues, and told her what Ernie had said in his report!

In June 1940, the Millen family made a serious mistake, moving to Brampton Road near the docks and, as a result of the London Blitz, were soon compelled to move out of the family home, with Ena taking their children, Jean and John, and evacuating them to Bromsgrove and then Horsham, whilst

Ernie was forced to sleep on the floor of the CID Office in which he worked.

In August 1941 Millen was transferred to the Murder Squad at Scotland Yard, where he met for the first time the man who was to play a large part in his career and who he would eventually succeed as Commander of the CID, George Hatherill.

After the War there was an outbreak of fraud, and between murder enquiries, Millen had busied himself in investigating some of them. As an educated man with a particular interest in mathematics, he started to make a name for himself in these enquiries, so that when he was promoted to Detective Sergeant 2nd class in early 1946 he was an obvious candidate for the newly-formed Fraud Squad.

When in the early hours of Saturday 15 May 1948 a call was received from Lancashire Police for the assistance of the Metropolitan Police in the case of the murder of a 4-year-old girl, June Anne Devaney, Detective Chief Inspector Jack (Charlie Artful) Capstick was selected with Millen, the first time that a Detective Sergeant 2nd Class had been selected for such a trip.

The case revolved around fingerprints found at the scene and Capstick required that all the men in the town of 120,000 people were fingerprinted, the first time that this had been done. Of course, the fact that this was a deplorable case of a young girl being kidnapped from a hospital where she was a patient, indecently assaulted and brutally murdered, meant that there was less opposition than might have been expected at such a proposal.

The case of June Anne Devaney became the first in which fingerprints had proved the case, and the strength of fingerprint evidence was clearly established for the public and led to many more convictions in the years to come.

On the day set for the trial, the Sergeant-to-Inspector promotion examination was due to be held. Millen was due to sit the examination, but was in Lancashire rather than London, giving evidence. He sought, and was granted, exceptional permission to sit the examination in Lancashire, with a local senior officer invigilating him in order to ensure fair play. Millen failed the competitive examination in which the top candidates secure automatic promotion, but gained the 60% pass mark necessary for a qualifying pass, which meant that he had passed at the bottom of a pile of around a hundred officers waiting to be promoted. There was just a little resentment when Millen was the first person promoted to Detective Sergeant 1st Class a few weeks later and given the plum posting of the Flying Squad.

On 4 January 1960 Millen was transferred to the Research and Planning Department, recently created by the Commissioner, Sir Joseph Simpson, on the advice of his Commander of CID, George Hatherill. Six weeks later Millen was promoted to Detective Chief Superintendent and it was proposed to transfer him to 3 District Headquarters, but this did not suit Millen geographically or intellectually and he made representations that resulted in him staying put, passing his time giving lectures on the work of the CID until an alternative posting that suited him better became available. The Metropolitan Police is a disciplined organisation and officers, particularly those at the top who get paid the most, are expected to go where they are sent, but Millen seems to have been receiving special treatment.

In his autobiography *Specialist in Crime*, reflecting his earlier interest in becoming a doctor, Millen records that in June 1961 he was transferred from the Force Research and Planning Department to the post of Head of the Flying Squad whilst on holiday in Looe in Cornwall. He then goes on to record his greatest achievement as head of the squad of the greatest detectives at Scotland Yard, men who focus on dealing with the most serious criminals in the country, often having to resort to the use of firearms to defend themselves against deadly force. Apparently, according to his autobiography, he reorganised the typing pool and introduced Dictaphones to save time and money.

Clearly Millen was of above average intelligence for a Police Officer of his time and he exercised excellent management skills, but he was not a great thief taker in the way that his subordinate, Tommy Butler, was. As a fraud investigator, he frequently spent many months on a single investigation, wading through piles of bank statements and seldom leaving the office, only to find that, at the last minute, the suspect had produced a medical certificate to certify that he was unfit to stand trial.

It took Millen twelve years to be promoted from Detective Constable to Detective Sergeant 2nd Class, and three years to be promoted from DS 2nd Class to DS 1st Class, he was then promoted from DS 1st Class to Assistant Commander in the ten years before the Great Train Robbery, an average of a promotion every second year, which is pretty good going. This period coincided with his meeting with George Hatherill. Clearly Hatherill and Commissioner Sir Joseph Simpson were impressed with his education and skills.

There is a 'golden rule' in the Metropolitan Police CID that every posting at a Scotland Yard Squad should be followed by a divisional posting, but somehow Millen managed to avoid this rule completely, so that from the time that he finished his first posting at Arbour Square in August 1941 until he retired as a Deputy Assistant Commissioner in 1969, he never worked on division: a series of ten postings in twenty-eight years.

Millen was known by his nickname of 'Hooter', which could have been because of the size of his nose, or for the way in which he eschewed the use of telephones to summon subordinates in nearby offices.

At the time of the Great Train Robbery, the man known as 'the World's Greatest Detective', Reg Spooner, was in hospital and died a few weeks later. It is likely that at the time of the robbery, his death may have been anticipated by the Commissioner and his fellow managers, including Hatherill, and that they had already earmarked Millen to take over from him, and that this is the reason why Millen was replaced by Butler so soon after his appointment to lead the enquiry.

Millen was the person who made the calamitous decision to circulate the names and photographs of the Great Train Robbers and their wives to the Press. Tommy Butler and Frank Williams, who were in charge of the enquiry, vehemently opposed this decision but were overruled by Millen, supported by Hatherill.

It has been claimed on Millen's behalf that he was more used to pursuing businessmen for Fraud, than Armed Robbers. His many opponents claim that Millen was a politician and strongly felt the pressure applied by the Prime Minister, the Home Secretary, the Postmaster General, British Rail and the Press, and also felt that he could beat Butler and Williams to claim credit for solving the 'Crime of the Century' by publishing the list of names of those suspected of the robbery.

Whichever explanation is true, Butler and Williams were right in claiming that publication would set desperate robbers, loaded with pockets full of cash, off all over the world in attempts to escape justice and extend the time that it would take to bring them to justice.

It was shortly after the robbery, on 1 October 1963, that Millen was promoted to Assistant Commander of the CID. In the next year, Hatherill was promoted and Millen was promoted to Commander of the CID, to replace him. In 1968 the CID was reorganised and Millen's position was re-graded to Deputy Assistant Commissioner (Administration). He retired from the Metropolitan Police in 1969.

Detective Chief Superintendent Tommy Butler

Tommy Butler was Head of the Metropolitan Police Flying Squad and the detective in charge of the team which investigated the Great Train Robbery.

Shepherd's Bush in West London developed as a town at the end of the late nineteenth and early twentieth century as shepherds stopped to pasture their animals on the way to selling them at Smithfield Market in Central London. The opening of Shepherd's Bush Station on the Metropolitan Railway in 1864 made it possible, for the first time, to commute to Central London, and opened the area to residential development.

Entertainment then became the local industry with the opening of the Shepherd's Bush Empire and the visit of Charlie Chaplin in 1903, the hosting of the Olympic Games and the Franco-British Exhibition in 1908, the construction of Lime Green Studios and the establishment of the British Broadcasting Corporation (BBC) in the area in 1915.

It was into this thriving, vibrant community, that the young Thomas Marius Joseph Butler was born on 21 July 1912. When he was just two years old the First World War broke out, and his father would have been called up to join the Army or one of the other armed forces. Things would have been tight until the end of the war four years later, although this war, unlike the one that followed, was fought in France, Belgium and Germany, rather than in England.

At the end of the 1920s and the early 1930s the world succumbed to the Great Depression, when the US Stock Exchange collapsed, international trade plunged by more than 50%, and unemployment rose as high as 33%, so that personal income, tax revenue, profits and prices all dropped throughout the world.

Police recruitment has always risen during a recession and it was in this climate that in 1934 the 22-year-old Tommy Butler applied to join the Metropolitan Police. This is interesting for a number of reasons. Young men were eligible to join the Police at age 20, so he was not in a hurry to join the force. At this time, women joined the "Women Police" a separate organisation, under separate management. There were 100 women covering the entire Metropolitan Police District, over all shifts. At each Police Station, Police Women had their own office and their own car and driver (male recruits had to achieve the rank of Chief Superintendent before they received similar perks! and worked entirely on dealing with women and children). At this time, senior officers were seeking men from outside London, above 5'9" in height, and preferably from strong farming stock, so that they could subdue criminals and deliver them, against their will, to the local Police station. There were no mobile telephones, personal radios, Police vans or cars in those days and somnolent drunks were conveyed to the station on a handcart.

The application and selection process for the Metropolitan Police in 1921 (thirteen years before Tommy Butler joined) was described by Detective Superintendent Robert Fabian in his book *Fabian of the Yard* (1950):

'A few days (after expressing an interest in joining) I received a Form A1/R8, which told me that I should be of British birth and pure British decent; over twenty but under twenty-seven; be 5'9" tall in my bare feet; able to read and show reasonable proficiency in writing from dictation and simple arithmetic. A stiff medical followed, at which I was able to assure them that, among other things, I had never been ruptured, nor suffered from flat feet, tumours or deformities of the face.'

Deputy Assistant Commissioner Ian Forbes, who joined the Metropolitan Police in 1938, confirmed in his book *Squadman* (1973) that there had been few changes in the selection and training of recruits between 1920 and 1938 and described the difficulty in gaining selection very clearly:

> 'I was one of eighty-five applicants from all over the United Kingdom, Eire and the Commonwealth – and fifteen of us were selected for service. Nine were offered the short-term, ten year contract (which went out of existence just before the outbreak of war in 1939) and I was among the six who were selected for the thirty year contract.'

Tommy Butler was not what you would describe as physically imposing. He was 5'9¼" tall, ten stone dripping wet, and best described as 'wiry'. He did not smoke and he drank alcohol only sparingly and described his education as 'elementary'. He was, however, focused, ambitious and prepared to work as hard as was necessary in order to achieve his ambitions. Despite several recorded instances of potential recruits of similar height and weight being rejected at this time, Tommy Butler was accepted and joined the Metropolitan Police on 22 October 1934. Perhaps the senior officers who interviewed him identified some of the qualities that later made him the detective that he would become.

At the time of joining the Metropolitan Police the young Police Constable Butler recorded that he lived with his widowed mother at 41 Washington Road in Barnes, London SW13, in the London Borough of Richmond, less than two and a half miles south of where he had been born, and was employed as a warehousemen.

Upon joining the Metropolitan Police, he would have had to report to Scotland Yard to be sworn in by the Commissioner, his deputy or one of his four assistants. He would then have been either marched or bussed to Peel House in Regency Street, situated between Victoria Station and Vauxhall Bridge, for ten weeks initial training, which would have included rote learning, large quantities of physical training, drill, boxing, self-defence and first aid.

Life at Training School was vividly described by Detective Chief Superintendent Arthur Thorp in his book *Calling Scotland Yard* (1954):

'Ten weeks I spent there, ten tough weeks of short haircuts, white stiff collars, stiff discipline and lessons in everything from spelling to the counterfeiter's art. Yes, spelling. In those days the educational standard of many of the recruits was extremely low, as the authorities of the day, rightly or wrongly (it's an arguable point) placed greater emphasis on physical condition than on learning. It seemed that they were looking for brawn rather than brains. And when they got their muscle they devoted considerable pains to making it tougher still, and just a little bit brighter. I revelled in it all – the boxing and wrestling in particular.'

Traditionally at this time young recruits were posted to Inner London Divisions, then transferred to semi-Inner London Divisions upon marriage, and again to Outer London Divisions when they had children. Only when there were shortages of manpower were these policies varied. Tommy Butler was posted to K Division in the East End of London, as P.C. 965 K and sent to live at the Canning Town Section House. Clearly, K Division needed men.

Section house life was described by Detective Chief Superintendent Arthur Thorp in his book, *Calling Scotland Yard*:

'Our rooms at Hammersmith (Section House) consisted of bleak and bare cubicles, separated by seven-foot partitions and lit by hissing, popping gas lamps suspended so that they served for two cubicles – and part of the corridor – at a time. They were always switched off abruptly at midnight, leaving us to study, as we had to, by the glimmer of forbidden candles. The wash rooms and lavatories were rough and ready, to say the least of them, and usually were constructed of cold, grey stone. The mess room was rather like that in a gaol, with rows of scrubbed deal tables and backless benches. There were no trimmings anywhere in the place and I can't say that anyone there would have wanted any.'

Working twenty miles away from his mother and living in a Section House fifteen miles away from her, did not suit the young Tommy and he started campaigning for a transfer closer to home, but not too close, as Barnes is a very quiet crime-free area, so he applied for a transfer to F Division covering Hammersmith and Fulham, close enough to live at home with his mother, but also a good area for an ambitious young police officer to learn his trade.

At this time Police Regulations required all young officers to live in the Police Section House until they got married and could apply to move to Police Married Quarters or to their own premises, which few could afford. These officers would be expected to wear uniform, (minus their duty armband) and act as a constant reserve so that they could be called upon when necessary). Tommy must have submitted an application to his Chief Superintendent to be exempted from these regulations on compassionate grounds, so that he could be with his widowed mother. As frequent checks were made at this time, it must be assumed that this authority was granted.

Once settled on F Division, the new PC 349 F set about gaining experience and completing his two-year probationary period. In his final probationary examination he achieved 85% and was awarded honours. He was starting to earn the sobriquets that accompanied him throughout his Police service, "One Day Tommy", "The Grey Fox", "Mr Flying Squad", and, with his friend and colleague, Jasper Peter Vibart, "The Terrible Twins".

He then applied for, and was selected to, appointment as an 'aid to CID'. This meant that he would transfer to plain clothes patrol duties and be subject to CID rather than uniformed management. He would be available to assist with major enquiries such as murders and have the opportunity to shine and secure selection to become a detective constable and full member of the Criminal Investigation Department. Tommy could now wear his own clothes while at work, but he would need to secure selection to the CID before he could throw away his uniform and wear plain clothes for the rest of his service.

Tommy Butler was now doing what he wanted to do, where he wanted to do it and he set about making his mark. He quickly received two Commissioner's Commendations, for 'sagacity in a case of larceny' and for 'zeal in a case of attempted larceny'. Larceny is an old-fashioned word for theft.

In March 1938 Tommy achieved his ambition of becoming a detective and was appointed to the rank of Detective Constable (DC). He was posted to West End Central Police Station, covering the areas of Mayfair, with its rich and famous, and Soho, with its vice and sex, but still only six miles from his home in Barnes. The work that he would be dealing with here would be considerably different to that which he was used to at F District, with few local residents in the West End but very large transient populations changing day-by-day. As a DC he would be working from the CID office investigating crimes.

In September 1941, just as the new West End Central Police Station at 27 Saville Row, London W1, alongside London's tailoring community, opened, Tommy was transferred to the Metropolitan Police Flying Squad (COC8) at Scotland Yard, the home of the best detectives, responsible for cultivating the best informants, solving the best crimes, and arresting the best criminals all over London.

As a member of the Flying Squad, aged less than thirty and with less than seven years' service, Tommy Butler was in the right place, but the Second World War was under way and conscription was in full swing and he could have been called up at any time.

The type of work undertaken by the Flying Squad at that time is, perhaps, best illustrated by the case of what an Old Bailey Judge called "The Battle of Heathrow". In 1948, Jack (Spot) Comer, a Polish immigrant and senior figure in the London Underworld, set up a plan to steal £1.5M worth of gold bullion and valuables from a warehouse at London's Heathrow Airport. This would have placed it on a par with the value of the Great Train Robbery fifteen years later.

The plan was for the robbers to infiltrate the guards and deliver drugged cups of teas to them, so that the gang of robbers could enter freely and steal the property. The Flying Squad received information from an informant so that officers were able to replace the entire team of guards, pretend to be asleep, and then ambush the robbers.

The fight that followed was extremely violent with the robbers assaulting the officers with iron bars, determined to steal the gold, and after they had arrested the robbers and locked them up, many of the officers were detained in hospital with serious injuries. This was not the type of work that Tommy Butler was built for. Every member of the gang of robbers was arrested and they received an average of 10 years imprisonment each and the Judge commended the Flying Squad officers for their work.

Tommy Butler would have found the Flying Squad a great place for a young, ambitious detective to learn the advanced skills of his profession. Detective Chief Superintendent Peter Beveridge had recently taken over the squad and selected five very strong Detective Inspectors to lead each of the teams, Jack Capstick, Ted Greeno, Alf Dance, John Ball and John Black.

A certain resentment was felt in some quarters against police officers who had stayed home rather than going away to fight in the war, and accordingly commendations were reserved to only the most deserving of cases, but Tommy Butler maintained a steady flow through the war years for:

"Promptitude, perseverance and ability in a case of Receiving"
"Ability and persistence in a difficult case under the Food Orders and Defence Regulations"
"Acumen and discretion in a case of Larceny and Receiving"
"Ability and perseverance in a case of Receiving"
"Vigilance and initiative in a case of Warehousebreaking"
"Ability and prudence in a case of Forgery"
"Perseverance and industry in a case of Receiving"
"Persistence and ability in a case of Conspiracy and Larceny"
"Diligence in a case of Housebreaking"
"Skill in a case of Receiving"
"Good work in a case of Storebreaking and Receiving"
"Skill in a case of Larceny and Conspiracy to Receive Stolen Goods"
"Zeal in a case of Receiving"

Detective Superintendent Gerald McArthur MBE QPM
Detective Superintendent Gerald McArthur was the forgotten man in the enquiry into the Great Train Robbery.

On 8 August 1963 the Chief Constable of the local Buckinghamshire Constabulary, Brigadier Cheney, seeking officers to lead the enquiry into the robbery, put in a call to George Hatherill, the Commander of the Criminal Investigation Department at Scotland Yard, before lunch time on the day of the robbery. Hatherill, despite having the 26,000 officers of the Metropolitan Police at his disposal, struggled to find a suitable investigating officer to take on what was already clearly a very serious crime, although it would be another couple of days before the full scale of the crime would become known.

Sir Richard Jackson, Hatherill's boss and the Assistant Commissioner (Crime) had taken one of the Deputy Commanders to the Interpol Conference in Finland. The other Deputy Commander, Reg Spooner, was terminally ill in hospital. Normal procedure was for a Detective Superintendent from the C1 Murder Squad to been sent to support Provincial Police Forces seeking assistance, but five out of the six of these men were already engaged in provincial murder enquiries. The next place to look was at the four Area Detective Superintendents, but three of these had also been sent out to investigate provincial murders. August is also the holiday season and some of the suitable candidates were away on holiday. This is not to say that Gerald McArthur was not an excellent candidate.

A conference on the robbery had been arranged for the afternoon at the GPO in London, and Hatherill agreed to attend and to take Detective Chief Superintendent Ernie Millen, the Head of the Flying Squad, and Detective Superintendent Gerald McArthur, his appointed Investigating Officer, so that they could meet the officers from the Buckinghamshire Constabulary, the British Transport Police and the Post Office Investigations Branch, who had conducted the early investigations into the robbery, so that they could catch up.

A detective working in a new area has many priorities, to find an office, a desk, a telephone, to meet his new boss, his new colleagues, to find out what has happened and what needs to be done, to find somewhere to live, somewhere to eat and report back to his bosses at home. In a case like the Great Train Robbery, there are also the small matters of press interest and calls from the public attempting to help with information that will block up switchboards and even access to the Police Station.

After two days, and with pressure mounting to achieve results, Hatherill reviewed the arrangements that he had made. Suspects had been identified and it had become clear that the robbery had been conducted by a South London team, so Hatherill decided to transfer the enquiry back to London and to give it to the Flying Squad, who specialised in dealing with armed robbers. With his deputy, Reg Spooner, terminally ill in hospital, Hatherill decided to promote Detective Chief Superintendent Ernie Millen to Deputy Commander and to recall Detective Chief Superintendent Tommy Butler, who had recently been transferred out of the Flying Squad on promotion.

Hatherill then decided to soothe any potential resentment in Buckinghamshire by arranging for their CID Chief, Detective Superintendent Malcolm Fewtrell to receive all prisoners and to deal with all related correspondence and press enquiries. Finally, Detective Superintendent Gerald McArthur was deputed to collate and assess all the statements and evidence in the case, a vital but low profile role. He spent nine months on the case, missing his wedding anniversary and putting his family up at a hotel so he could be with them at Christmas, but his meticulous methods earned the convictions that he had been sent to secure.

Gerald McArthur was born on 28 May 1916 in Newport in Gwent. He captained the Welsh Schoolboys at rugby and retained a life-long interest in sport, latterly playing bowls. Despite an early interest in becoming an architect, he joined the Metropolitan Police in 1935, as soon as he was eligible. He completed his probation, a period as an 'aid to CID' and a posting as a Detective Constable before being transferred to Scotland Yard in 1941. Then, secure in his future, he married in the same year, going on to have two daughters. Later, he served with the RAF as a pilot in Coastal Command during the Second World War, achieving the rank of Flight Lieutenant. After the War, McArthur rejoined Scotland Yard and by the time of the Robbery had worked his way up to the rank of Detective Superintendent.

The sheer scale of the Great Train Robbery made it obvious that provincial police forces at that time were not equipped to investigate major crimes. In 1964 Parliament passed the Police Act, which re-organised force boundaries and reduced the number of small forces, so that Buckinghamshire Constabulary became part of Thames Valley Police, and established Regional Crime Squads, which worked across force boundaries. Gerald McArthur was the obvious candidate for the post of Coordinator of the No.5 Squad, with the rank of Temporary Assistant Chief Constable. It was in this capacity that he began a painstaking investigation into the activities of the Richardson gang, rivals to the Krays, who ruled East London on the other side of the Thames. The Richardsons had built up a lucrative empire by extortion, fraud, and torture, which included beatings and electric shocks. More often than not, henchman 'Mad' Frankie Fraser was responsible for the worst of the violence. At the time, corruption was rife in the Metropolitan Police, but due to McArthur's reputation for being dead straight, and the fact that he was divorced from Scotland Yard in his new role, witnesses came forward, and he secured a twenty-five year sentence for Charles Richardson and a ten-year sentence for his brother Eddie Richardson. 'Mad' Frankie Fraser and Roy Hall were also sent down.

In his long and distinguished service with the Police, Gerald McArthur was awarded the Queen's Police Medal and received thirty-three commendations. He also gained a reputation as 'one of the finest detectives of his generation'.

On his retirement he worked as a Security Adviser to the Tobacco Advisory Council, but he never lost his links with his former colleagues. Gerald McArthur died on 21 July 1995.

Detective Superintendent Ernest Malcolm Fewtrell

Malcolm Fewtrell was the Head of the Criminal Investigation Department (CID) in Buckinghamshire Constabulary, who was summoned from his bed at 4.30 a.m. on 8 August 1963 to be told that there had been a train robbery at Cheddington. He arrived at the scene at 5.00 am to take charge of the 'Crime of the Century' only to have it taken away from him around noon the same day, when his Chief Constable handed the investigation over to the Metropolitan Police.

After taking note of the thieves' efficiency, he supervised the gathering of such evidence as a bloody cloth and the coupling on the mail coach of the train. Next he went to Cheddington Station, where he supervised statements being taken from more than eighty people on the train, including the coshed driver. These confirmed that about fifteen hooded men had been involved, but little else.

It was during the taking of these statements that Fewtrell made the first of two mistakes that delayed the enquiry and caused friction with the Metropolitan Police Officers who soon assumed responsibility for the enquiry. He picked up on the fact that the robbers had told the Post Office personnel on the train to stay inside for thirty minutes after the robbery as they would leave people outside to 'deal with them' if they tried to escape and call for help. He concluded that the robbers had realised that roadblocks would be set up as soon as the Police heard about the robbery, and that instead of running back to London, they had probably gone to ground within thirty miles of the robbery. Accordingly, he instigated a search of all premises within thirty miles of the scene.

It is natural to start such a search at the scene and work outwards, and this is what Fewtrell did. However, when the experienced Scotland Yard detectives arrived to take over the enquiry, they were outraged that the search had been started at the scene and worked outwards. They realised that there was no chance that the thieves had hidden at the end of the road and that they would have run as far away from the scene as they felt able in the time available, and that the search should have started at the thirty-mile boundary and worked back to the scene. This decision delayed the finding of the hideout until the robbers had cleaned up and left.

By lunchtime it was clear that the Buckinghamshire force did not have the necessary resources to conduct the enquiry and Fewtrell advised his Chief Constable to call in Scotland Yard. A conference was arranged for 3.00 pm on the day of the robbery at the GPO offices in London, where the officers from Buckinghamshire, the British Transport Police and the Post Office Investigations Branch would set out the facts for the Metropolitan Police, who were taking over the enquiry. At the end of the meeting Malcolm Fewtrell handed over the enquiry to Detective Superintendent Gerald McArthur of the Met.

The handover of the case did not stop calls and letters containing information from the public and press enquiries arriving in Buckinghamshire, and Fewtrell and his officers continued to deal with it.

The second problem arose when Detective Superintendent John Cummings, Head of the Criminal Intelligence Department at Scotland Yard, complained that his informant 'Mickey' told him that the robbers were in a farmhouse and that they would leave the farm the next day. Cummings passed the information to Fewtrell while he was leading the enquiry, but no action was taken. Fewtrell claimed that he did not have enough manpower to search all the local farms. Then a few days later when, as a result of further information, the Police did search Leatherslade Farm, they found that the robbers had fled, leaving mailbags stuffed with bank wrappers and Post Office chits, clearly from the train, and a considerable stock of food.

In the course of the enquiry Fewtrell was asked to interview the solicitors' clerk, Brian Field, who had helped the robbers to buy Leatherslade Farm, and who was suspected of being the 'Mr Field' named on a German hotel bill found with a stash of the money in Reigate, Surrey. Fewtrell trapped him, over a cup of tea, into admitting responsibility for the bill.

Later, as part of his responsibility for the prisoners, he was responsibility for the security of the makeshift court room in the Aylesbury District Council offices, and for £300,000 which were shown to be proceeds of the robbery and which had to be held as evidence.

Fewtrell's main responsibility was more nebulous than the others. He had to ensure that his officers cooperated with the Metropolitan Police officers working at his police station in close proximity to his officers. He needed to ensure that the natural feelings that 'big brother' had moved in and taken over and that their professionalism was being questioned by their own Chief Constable, were controlled, and to ensure that officers from both police forces co-operated

Ernest Malcolm Fewtrell was born on 28 September 1909 in the Police house at Ryde on the Isle of Wight, one of six sons of a local Police Officer, four of whom became Police Officers themselves. He attended Reading School, then spent six months in New South Wales, Australia working as a jackaroo on sheep stations. He then returned to the UK and became a police cadet with Buckinghamshire Constabulary. When he achieved the age of 19, he graduated to becoming a Police Constable and his first posting was to Chesham. When he went into hospital with appendicitis he met and married a nurse, Anne Thomas, with whom he had a son and a daughter.

As a police officer Fewtrell was exempt from conscription, but was entitled to volunteer for military service in the Second World War. He was strongly advised by his superiors in the force not to do so and rose through the ranks, in both the uniformed and detective branches, reaching the rank of Detective Inspector by 1950 and Superintendent by 1954.

Around 1962 he was involved in the James Hanratty murder investigation, where he was given the task of assembling ten red-headed men for an identity parade, which necessitated borrowing several servicemen from a local RAF station.

At the time of the Great Train Robbery, Fewtrell was two weeks short of his 54th birthday. He had completed thirty-five years service, more than enough to qualify for a full Police pension. He had been giving serious thought to retiring, to focus on his family and his hobbies, but he chose to stay on in the force.

When Fewtrell did retire from the Police, shortly after the robbers' trial, he became the first Police Officer freed from Police Regulations to tell his side of the story. With the help of Ronald Payne, who was brought back from Moscow by *The Sunday Telegraph* to cover the case, he wrote *The Train Robbers* (1964). The book contained a summary of the facts, together with reflections on Post Office complacency and the confusion resulting from so many Police Officers working on one case. While paying tribute to individual Yard officers, he pointed out their variability: 'Some are first class, others not so good, and there are others still who just like to bask in the glory of being from Scotland Yard.'

On leaving the police, he took employment as an accommodation officer for Portsmouth Polytechnic before settling in Swanage, where he was a keen gardener. He relished the edition of The Complete Works of Dickens that he was given on his 80th birthday; he read it from front to back and then started again. He also took on the administration of the Neighbourhood Watch and continued to play golf into his nineties.

Fewtrell took the personal publicity connected with the train robbery in his stride, bluntly telling reporters he did not know why some people called him 'Maigret'. Long after his retirement, it was noted that he had a resemblance to John Thaw in *Morse*, the television series about a Detective Chief Inspector in the Thames Valley Police, the successor to the Buckinghamshire Constabulary that he had served so well. He died on 28 November 2005 aged 96.

Detective Chief Inspector Jasper Peter Vibart

Detective Chief Inspector Peter Vibart was assistant to DCS Ernie Millen with the main Robbery enquiry. He was a very tough operator. An ex-soldier, he joined the Metropolitan Police in 1936 and throughout his career he specialised in arresting the most violent men and delivering them to police stations. With Tommy Butler, they gained the sobriquet, 'The Terrible Twins'.

On 2 May 1956, the self-proclaimed 'King of the Underworld', Jack Spot, was seriously assaulted so as to require seventy-eight stitches to his face. Billy Hill was suspected of instigating the attack, but was alibied and released. Two of the attackers, 'Mad' Frankie Fraser and Bobby Warren, were convicted and sentenced to seven years imprisonment. Two of the other attackers, Bert 'Battles' Rossi and William 'Billy Boy' Blythe, were arrested in Dublin and the Metropolitan Police were contacted and invited to collect them.

Blythe had cut Vibart's face in 1945 so that he required twenty stitches, and there was little love lost between the two men. The barrister representing Rossi and Blythe, Patrick Marrinen, rushed from London to Dublin to complain that the warrants for the two men were flawed. The suspects were upset to be met by the Terrible Twins. Vibart used 'enough' force to detain Blythe and Rossi (few would have been brave enough to challenge him on the issue). Butler made complaints against Marrinem that caused him to be disbarred by the Bar Council.

On 29 March 1958, Police Constable Henry Stevens, an aide to CID on P Division, was shot in the mouth by Ronald Leonard Easterbrook, an armed robber and an exceptionally violent man. Despite his grievous injuries, Stevens held on to Easterbrook for a long time, before he eventually escaped. Enquiries revealed that Easterbrook was also wanted for two other offences of Grievous Bodily Harm. Easterbrook then went around South London pronouncing that he had another gun and that it contained five bullets for the first policemen that he saw and that the last one would prevent him from being taken alive. This was a challenge that Vibart found difficult to resist.

On 10 April 1958, Vibart went to the Goodwood Hotel, Queensborough Terrace, Bayswater. Finding the room barricaded and Easterbrook inside pointing a Colt .455 revolver at him, Vibart lost his temper, demolished the room and crushed his opponent.

Vibart was awarded thirty-four commendations, mostly for arresting violent men, but also for the investigation and arrest of the Chief Constable of Brighton and for the investigation of Colonel Grivas in Cyprus. Vibart simply did not know fear.

He retired from the Metropolitan Police with the rank of Detective Chief Superintendent.

The Flying Squad Investigation Team

Detective Inspector Frank Williams

At the time of the Robbery, Frank Williams was staying at the Royal Hotel in Cattolica, Italy with his family, on their annual holiday. The Italian Press gave extensive coverage to the Great Train Robbery and as the Detective Inspector in charge of 5 Squad of the Metropolitan Police Flying Squad, Frank Williams lapped up all the information that he could gather; and whilst still in Italy and without any access to his official files, he remembered the frequent trips made by the South West Gang to Buckinghamshire in recent months and correctly named the majority of those responsible for the Great Train Robbery.

Upon his return to work Frank Williams ran his theories past the other members of his 5 Squad and confirmed the details with them. When Tommy Butler was selecting the team that he wanted to assist him in the investigation of the robbery he chose Williams, describing him as the 'best informed detective at Scotland Yard' particularly on South London criminals. As the second in charge of the enquiry, Williams managed the squad investigating the robbery under the strategic direction of Butler.

Williams was a tough, grim-looking man with a pitted, pudgy face, seldom seen without a cigarette. Having seen active service as a Staff Sergeant in the Royal Marine Commandos, he had a reputation as a tough but fair man; a very quiet man who was frequently deep in thought. Williams was generally disapproved of by his Scotland Yard superiors for his unorthodox methods, had the reputation of being an undisciplined detective and regularly faced accusations of bribery, blackmail and corruption.

DI Williams had actively sought out and developed confidential informants whilst employed as a detective in South London. This is a skill which young detectives are encouraged to develop by their seniors and on which they are specifically assessed, as it develops their communication skills and extends their knowledge of crime and criminals. The management of informants also requires considerable political skills in order to persuade informants to supply information on the most serious and most violent thieves and then to deflect the suspicion of those who are frantically trying to work out who 'grassed' on them.

Williams developed a complex network of informants and grasses, and sought to corroborate all the information that he received, through duplicate sources. During the enquiry he maintained several open lines of communication with each of the outstanding suspects.

The most successful informant handlers achieve outstanding results in terms of the number and quality of their arrests, but their senior officers, who have no opportunity to supervise the relationships of their subordinates, are always deeply worried by them and suspect that the results are perhaps 'too good' and wonder what deals have been done in order to secure them.

One of Frank Williams' closest criminal contacts was Freddy Foreman, who ran a pub on Williams' patch in Kennington.

Foreman was a Kray henchman and holds the record for acquittals for murder at the Old Bailey, with four. He has since published biographical books admitting responsibility for various murders, such as that of Frank Mitchell, 'the Mad Axe Man', who was sprung from prison on the orders of the Kray Brothers but who then became an embarrassment to them.

Williams' successes lead to his selection for the Flying Squad and subsequently to his promotion to Detective Chief Superintendent. However, his negotiations with Foreman that led to the recovery of £50,000 of the proceeds of the Robbery, an attempt to secure a second such recovery and the arrest of Buster Edwards, which Williams felt would secure him the job that he craved, ultimately led to his rejection for the post and his retirement from the Metropolitan Police, and a job as Head of Security at Qantas Airlines.

Throughout the Robbery enquiry, Williams was partnered by Detective Sergeant Steve Moore.

Detective Sergeant Stanley (Steve) Moore

Stanley (Steve) Moore was a very pleasant and well-spoken man who got on well with all those who he worked with. He joined the Flying Squad in September 1960 as a Detective Sergeant (2nd Class) and was posted to 5 Squad. In 1962 the Squad received information that three armed men were going to rob the Midland Bank in Kingsbury Road, Kingsbury Green as it opened. Frank Williams, Steve Moore and other 5 Squad officers waited in a nondescript van outside the bank.

As the bank opened three men arrived at the front door, covered their faces with masks and pulled out handguns. Two were immediately arrested, but the third ran off with Steve Moore in hot pursuit. Michael Hampshire then turned and fired the pistol at Moore, but this did not stop him. As the two men arrived in nearby Slough Lane, Hampshire jumped into a waiting getaway car and slammed the door behind him. Moore opened the door and Hampshire took careful aim at his head, but the driver accelerated sharply and the shot missed Moore. The officer held on to the vehicle for a while before he was thrown off at a corner.

During the pursuit Moore's suit was shredded and he endured considerable jesting from his colleagues. He was also sternly rebuked by his wife when he got home, probably as she realised that he could easily have been similarly damaged. However, his day improved considerably when the Squad received information that Hampshire was drinking in a public house in Golders Green. It got better still when he heard that Hampshire had made the mistake of resisting arrest when the officers arrived!

Later, at the Old Bailey, Hampshire was sentenced to three and a half year's imprisonment whilst Moore was Highly Commended by the Commissioner. He was also awarded a token £20 from the prestigious Bow Street Fund.

Following the conviction of the Great Train Robbers, Frank Williams was posted off the Flying Squad in order to secure the experience that would, in due course, secure him the promotions that he sought (a phrase that was to be repeatedly cited on the personnel files of officers on the Flying Squad). He was replaced as the leader of 5 Squad by Detective Inspector Jim Barnett.

There was something of a crime wave in the UK in 1964 and the Home Office responded by setting up the Regional Crime Squad with five branch offices across London, in opposition to the Flying Squad.

Two armed robbers, Mark Owen and Freddie Sanson, had made themselves busy attacking banks across South London in recent months and were regularly firing their weapons, making it likely that they would eventually kill or seriously injure members of the public. An interesting feature of their partnership was that whilst Sanson was white, Owen was black, making them a mixed race team and, as such, unique amongst robbery teams at this time.

One evening the Squad received information that at 10 pm Owen and Sanson would be in the vicinity of the Oval Cricket Ground in Kennington. Barnett took 5 Squad, including Moore, down there to search for them. Once on the plot, Moore spotted Owen and chased after him. Remembering that Owen had been described as 'armed and dangerous', Moore drew his truncheon and for the first and only time in his career, used it. He hit

Owen over the head so hard that the truncheon 'bounced' off it. Shortly afterwards, Sanson was arrested at home in bed. Later, at the Old Bailey, Owen was awarded ten years imprisonment and Sanson fifteen years.

Steve Moore left the Squad after seven years, to secure the experience that he required to secure the promotions that he sought, but in 1975 he was working on attachment at the Home Office when he received information that an attempt would be made to rob the Bank of America in London's Mayfair. Moore contacted Commander Dave Dilley at C11, the Criminal Intelligence Branch at New Scotland Yard, who tasked Detective Inspector Trevor Lloyd-Hughes with the enquiry.

Although the officers correctly identified the robbers they erred on the time of the robbery and, employing a blend of electronic skills and explosives, the robbers broke into the bank and stole £8 million worth of cash, jewellery and contents of safety deposit boxes.

Seven men who took part in the £8 million robbery received gaol terms totalling nearly one hundred years. The mastermind behind the robbery, Frank Maple, left Britain shortly after the robbery and is believed to have gone to Morocco, which had no extradition treaty with the UK. At the Old Bailey, Judge King-Hamilton passed the longest sentences on those considered to be the ringleaders: safe-cracker Leonard Wilde was sent to 23 years imprisonment, and Peter Colson, a 32-year-old used car dealer, to 21 years imprisonment. Others in the gang were sentenced to periods ranging from eighteen years for robbery to three years for receiving stolen goods.

Steve Moore had retired from the Metropolitan Police with the rank of Detective Chief Superintendent at C11, the Criminal Intelligence Branch at New Scotland Yard. Today, half a century after the Great Train Robbery, he is the last surviving member of the team that investigated the robbery.

Detective Sergeant Jim Nevill

Jim Nevill was a seasoned, old-style detective, firm and authoritative; he was a tenacious investigator and interrogator, but fair-minded and likeable. These skills are always in demand and served him well whether he was investigating the Great

Train Robbery, chasing Georgi Markov, the Bulgarian who shot a ricin-coated pellet into his victim on Waterloo Bridge, or Carlos the International Terrorist, managing the Balcombe Street Siege or leading the Metropolitan Police Anti-Terrorist Branch.

James Francis Nevill was born on 20 February 1927 in Balham, near Clapham, in South London. On leaving school he became an engineer with a company making heavy munitions. The job inspired a lifelong interest in guns and ammunition, and he developed a marksman's eye, competing at Bisley and later serving as President of the Bisley Gun Club.

He spent much of his National Service in the Middle East with the Royal Fusiliers driving armoured cars, an experience that led him to toy briefly with the idea of becoming a professional rally driver. In the event he was discharged as a lance-corporal and returned to civilian life, working in the retail sector before joining the Metropolitan Police in 1948.

His first posting was to the police station at Rochester Row, and he was working as an aide to CID there when he met WPC Marion Nelson. They married in 1954, by which time Nevill had embarked on a career as a detective, starting in the Criminal Records Office (CRO) at Scotland Yard, where talented officers with potential were sent to gain experience.

A series of postings led to his joining the Flying Squad as a Detective Sergeant 2nd Class in the early 1960s, where he was hand-picked by Detective Chief Superintendent Tommy Butler to become one of the six man squad selected to investigate the Great Train Robbery in August 1963.

When in June 1974 the Provisional IRA bombed the Houses of Parliament, injuring eleven people, Nevill was head of the CID in London's A Division which covered that area. When the Deputy Assistant Commissioner, Ernie Bond, arrived at the scene, he immediately appointed Nevill to be number two to Commander Roy Habershon, Head of the Bomb Squad (later the Anti-Terrorist Squad). This was a period of intense IRA activity and in the course of the previous year they had launched some eighty-five bomb attacks on the UK mainland, resulting in nearly 400 casualties.

Three months later in October 1974 the IRA bombed two pubs used by military personnel at Guildford in Surrey, killing six and injuring thirty-five others. Once again Nevill was one of the first senior men on the scene. The case led to the conviction of four men, and a vociferous campaign for the 'Guildford Four' to be acquitted, which eventually happened in 1989.

Throughout 1975, Nevill frequently appeared on television as the IRA targeted the London Hilton Hotel as well as restaurants such as Scott's, Lockets and Walton's in a bombing campaign. In December of that year Nevill faced one of his toughest tests when a gang of four IRA gunmen whom he had been hunting were ambushed by Flying Squad detectives and chased through the streets in a running gun battle before holing up in a flat at Balcombe Street, not far from Marylebone Station and taking a middle-aged couple hostage for six days.

Psychologically, the Balcombe Street Siege began badly for the authorities, with the Metropolitan Police Commissioner Sir Robert Mark branding the gang as 'vulgar common criminals' and bluntly broadcasting that their only destination would be a cell at Brixton prison.

With his second-in-command, Peter Imbert, Nevill embarked on a cat-and-mouse game, ordering the telephone line to the flat to be cut, addressing the gang from the street through a loudhailer and offering them a field telephone (which was accepted) as a means of communicating with the police, so establishing procedures which form the basis of tactics for sieges to the present day.

Despite the nerve-racking circumstances, Nevill was relieved to discover that the terrorists, while heavily armed and undoubtedly ruthless, had a sense of humour. Inviting them to call him Jim, he was told by the gang – tongue-in-cheek – that their names were Tom, Mick and Paddy. Although it transpired that there were four of them rather than three, these were the names Nevill and his team used throughout the stand-off.

Pressure built up on the police and the terrorists (not to mention the hostages, John and Sheila Matthews) as the siege dragged on. On day five, after the destruction of the field telephone, which the terrorists had hurled from a window, Nevill left his command post in nearby Dorset Square to return to the street outside the flat with the loudhailer, trying to persuade the gang leader to allow food to be passed inside, which he eventually did.

During his halting 22-minute dialogue with 'Tom', Nevill sought to push the gang towards the end-game, carefully avoiding the use of the psychologically-negative word 'surrender'. Patient negotiation by Nevill and Imbert finally paid off when the gang gave up after six days and the hostages were freed unharmed. Throughout the incident Nevill appeared in television news reports night after night – unruffled and immaculate – as one of the two senior detectives negotiating with the cornered gang of renegade IRA gunmen.

The following year Nevill was promoted to Commander and put in charge of the Bomb Squad, whilst Imbert later became Commissioner of the Metropolitan Police.

Before his retirement Nevill was awarded the Queen's Police Medal.

During his five years as head of the Anti-Terrorist Squad, Nevill led the hunts for the international terrorist known as Carlos the Jackal, for the killer of Georgi Markov, assassinated at a London bus stop by a poisoned pellet fired from an umbrella, and led the investigation into the shooting of El Al staff at the Europa Hotel in Central London.

In 1979, having undergone heart bypass surgery at the age of 51, following years dealing with the stress of front-line policing, Nevill ended his 32-year career in the Metropolitan Police in charge of the CID in South London. One of his last tasks was to travel to Leeds to advise the West Yorkshire Police detectives on his experiences of handling some of the largest criminal investigations ever. Unfortunately, it was another twelve months before Peter Sutcliffe was arrested as a result of a stop in the street by two uniformed officers.

After a short rest, Nevill joined Barclays Bank in a senior security role the next year. He died on 12 December 2007, aged 80.

Detective Sergeant Jack Slipper

Jack Slipper was born in Ealing, Middlesex in April 1924. He attended Little Ealing School until the age of fourteen. From

1938 to 1941 he worked as an electrician's apprentice. Then, lying about his age, he enlisted in the Royal Air Force. From April 1941 to August 1943 he served as an electrician with a night fighter squadron in West Malling, Kent. In August 1943 he was posted to Rhodesia where he served until February 1946 as an electrician with an Air Training Group in Salisbury. From March 1946 he worked as an electrician at Haven Green, Ealing.

In April 1951, at the age of 27, Slipper decided to follow his brother and join the Police, but whereas his brother had joined the City of London Force, Jack decided that he wanted more action and decided to join the Metropolitan Police. After training at the Hendon Police College he was posted to Brentford as a uniformed constable, but after a few weeks there, he again decided that he needed more action and approached his Chief Inspector seeking a transfer to Central London. The Chief Inspector attempted to persuade Slipper that he had to stay, but Slipper produced the correct forms, correctly filled out in order to resign from the Force. Convinced now by Slipper's determination, the Chief Inspector reluctantly agreed to go away and make the necessary telephone calls. Thus it was that from December 1951 to May 1956 he was a constable in Chelsea. He then transferred to the CID and was a Detective Constable in Acton until January 1962, when he transferred to the Flying Squad.

Jack Slipper was attached to the Flying Squad from January 1962 to until January 1968, a period of six years, double the usual posting. In that time he was promoted from Detective Constable to Detective Sergeant 2nd Class in April 1962, to Detective Sergeant 1st Class in March 1964 and to Detective Inspector in July 1966. He played a key role in investigating two of the most serious crimes to have occurred in the twentieth century: the Great Train Robbery on 8 August 1963, and the Foxtrot One-One Incident at Shepherds Bush on 12 August 1966, when three CID officers were shot down and murdered in cold blood. For these six years, he probably did not achieve eight hours continuous sleep at any time.

In January 1968, he was transferred to Harlesden Division, in order to gain the Divisional experience that he needed to secure his next promotion. He was duly promoted to

Detective Chief Inspector in September 1968 and transferred to the headquarters of 'Q' Division in Wembley, where he was responsible for investigating complaints made against Police Officers, particularly any criminal complaints, due to his experience as a detective. He remained at Wembley until October 1971 when he was promoted to Detective Chief Superintendent and transferred to head the Stolen Car Squad at Chalk Farm.

It was whilst at the Stolen Car Squad that Slipper was selected to lead the team of Regional Crime Squad and Flying Squad Officers delegated to respond to a series of statements made by Bertie Smalls. Derek Creighton (Bertie) Smalls had been arrested for Armed Robbery at Barclays Bank in High Street, Wembley in 1972. After three months in custody awaiting trial, during which the Regional Crime Squad officers dealing with him had been reviewing all the other crimes that he had been committing, young Bertie decided that he was prepared to do whatever was necessary in order to avoid the considerable term of imprisonment that he was facing. He offered to tell the officers everything he knew about crimes, particularly armed robberies.

On 2 January, Smalls asked for a meeting with the lead Inspector. In the conversation, Smalls (having been informed by his solicitor that he would be serving at least twenty-five years if convicted) offered the police a deal to name and incriminate those involved not only in the Barclays Bank job but in every piece of criminal activity he had ever been involved with or known of. An agreement was drawn up between Smalls and the Director of Public Prosecutions, Sir Norman Skelhorn, that gave Smalls complete immunity from prosecution in exchange for his help. Jack Slipper was involved in his debriefing and subsequent handling.

On 11 February 1974 the trial commenced at the Old Bailey, Court No.2, of the Wembley Mob in relation to the Barclays Bank robbery. Smalls duly gave evidence and assisted the authorities. As he concluded his evidence against some of his former friends in one of the committal hearings, they sang to him the Vera Lynn song: *We'll meet again, don't know where, don't know when* ... On 20 May the trial finished, with the jury returning guilty verdicts on all participants on 22 May. In total the judge handed out sentences totalling 106 years, with Green alone jailed for 18 years. In the following fourteen months, Smalls' evidence convicted a further twenty-one associates for a total of 308 years. Smalls also later ensured the release of Jimmy Saunders, jailed by DCI Bert Wickstead for his part in the 1970 Ilford robbery, after a statement in which he said Saunders was not part of the gang.

The Smalls case was significant for three reasons: the first informer to give the police volume names of his associates and provide the evidence that would send dozens of them to prison to serve long sentences; the first criminal informer to strike a written deal with the Director of Public Prosecutions; the only criminal informer to serve no time for his crime in return for providing Queen's evidence.

In March 1973 Slipper returned to the Flying Squad as operational Chief Superintendent, returning to Wembley as Detective Chief Superintendent in January 1977.

He was returned to uniform duty on 4 January 1977, most probably due to his involvement in the case of Derek Creighton "Bertie" Smalls (1935–31 January 2008), Britain's first "supergrass", which came to a head in 1976. Slipper was in charge of Smalls' debriefing. Smalls provided evidence against most of the active armed robbers in Greater London, but the case brought criticism of the Director of Public Prosecutions (DPP) and the Metropolitan Police, when it was announced that the DPP had awarded Smalls total immunity from prosecution despite his involvement in a considerable number of armed robberies at banks and building societies.

He retired from police work in December 1979, after which he worked as a security consultant for IBM UK. He died in 2005, aged 81.

Detective Sergeant Lou Van Dyck

One of the six officers on the 'Special Enquiry Team' selected by Tommy Butler to investigate the Great Train Robbery, Lou van Dyck was another detective from the East End of London. He was a hugely charismatic figure and a great raconteur. When officers had occasion to make enquiries of the Jewish community, they would often be asked, 'Do you know Mr Louis?'

Van Dyke was a committed gambler and it is said that he lost his house in Upminster, Essex to pay off his gambling debts. He literally would bet on the outcome of two flies crawling up a wall. His funeral a few years ago was very well attended – he was a much admired figure in police circles.

After the Great Train Robbery investigation, he was posted to the Metropolitan Police Detective Training School at Peel House, in Regency Street, between Victoria Station and Vauxhall Bridge, in Central London, as a Detective Inspector.

By 1981 Lou van Dyke had been promoted to Detective Chief Superintendent and put in charge of the Met's K Division covering an area north of the River Thames from Plaistow in the east to Dagenham in the west.

As a matter of interest, every member of the squad achieved the rank of Detective Chief Superintendent.

Detective Constable Tommy Thorburn

Paired with Lou van Dyck, Tommy Thorburn was one of the six officers on the 'Special Enquiry Team'. In 1957, he was a Detective Constable working from Chadwell Heath Police Station, then part of K Division, when he received a telephone call from a resident of Donald Drive in Romford. The man was away from home, in Germany, on business and had asked a neighbour to keep an eye on his home while he was away. The neighbour had called him to report that there was a broken window at the rear of the premises.

When Thorburn went to investigate, he found the broken window. Of course, this did not mean that the premises had been burgled as the house was near a main road and it was entirely possible that the window had been broken by a stone thrown up by a passing vehicle. However, being a dedicated police officer, Thorburn decided to enter the premises through the broken window and have a look around. What he found caused him serious concern. More than fifty handguns, including Mausers and Lugers, all in working order.

This meant a great deal of work for Thorburn. A lazy officer would have walked past the guns and said nothing. Nobody would have ever known. All the weapons had to be taken to the police station, where they had to be listed in detail, with their serial numbers, placed in property bags and all the bag numbers recorded. Arrangements would then have to be made for all the weapons to be sent to the Metropolitan Police Laboratory to ensure that they had not been connected with any crime. Further enquiries would be required into the owner of the handguns and the ways in which each of the weapons had come into his possession. A report would then have to be made of all the details of the investigation before arranging for the weapons to be returned to the owner or disposed of.

Thorburn traced the owner of the weapons, John Hall, a married car salesman and a member of a local gun club. He was in his late twenties, 6'1" tall and stocky build. When he spoke to him, Thorburn discovered that Hall had an explosive temper, had previous convictions and, as a young man had spent time in an Approved School. He also discovered that Hall had been discharged from the Royal Air Force on the grounds of mental instability and that he had received treatment in a psychiatric hospital. Not exactly the type of person that you want possessing weapons.

Thorburn prepared a detailed report of his investigation for the information of Department S1 at New Scotland Yard, which had responsibility for the licensing of firearms and the prosecution of firearms offences. He proposed that the weapons should be confiscated, Hall's firearms certificate be cancelled, and consideration be given to prosecuting him. Instead he received a reply instructing him to return all weapons to Hall immediately and advising that no further action was considered appropriate. Clearly, the civilian staff at S1 did not have the stomach for a fight and the consequences of their incompetence would become clear in time.

Time passed. Hall divorced and remarried. He worked as a salesman for a car parts shop where, after a row with his employer, he resigned. When his employer reconciled the stock and cash in hand he identified a loss of £5, which he reported to the police. When he heard of the police investigation, Hall asked his new wife for a loan to cover the amount and when she refused it, he hit her over the head with a chair, causing a wound that required twenty-two stitches. When his mother-in-law took issue with his treatment of his wife, he broke her wrist and inflicted injures to her that required twenty-two stitches. He then assaulted his sister-in-law, but less seriously.

On Saturday 3 June 1961, at 1.05 pm, Hall responded to a call from police by attending West Ham Police Station to discuss the allegations against him. When the officers mentioned that they were intending to arrest him, Hall produced a Walther 9mm pistol from his trouser pocket, ran out of the station and down the road. He was pursued by several officers as he ran in and out of several private houses and down several roads. Inspector Pawsey, Sergeant Hutchins (who was only at the police station to be formally disciplined by a senior officer!) and Constable Cox received bullet wounds, before Hall shot himself in the head. Pawsey and Hutchins died, and Cox, though seriously injured, survived.

Tommy Thorburn was by now working from Dagenham Police Station. Working a split shift he was resting at home with a colleague and a cool drink, when he received the call informing him that he was required to deal with the shooting of three police officers. He dropped everything and hurried to work.

As hundreds of officers were posted to roadblocks and house searches, Thorburn reported his earlier investigation into Hall's possession of firearms and identified the weapon used to kill the officers as one of those returned to him by S1 Department.

The next day, Hall went to a telephone box at the junction of Lake House Road and Alderbrook Road in Wanstead, where he called the *Sunday Express* newspaper and explained to them who he was and what he had done. The journalists kept him talking while their colleagues called the police. Officers were sent to the scene, but when they got there they found that Hall had shot himself. They took him to hospital, and he was soon fit enough to be arrested and charged with his crimes.

Six days after their murder, on Friday 9 June 1961, the two deceased officers were buried at the City of London cemetery, Alderbrook Road, Manor Park and the next day, Hall suddenly collapsed and died.

Although in no way responsible for the return of the weapons, the angst of the situation haunted Tommy Thorburn for the rest of his life. He died in 2000.

Recollections of the Police Constables from Buckinghamshire Police

The following were the full statements of the officers produced for the 50th Anniversary of the Robbery, and are reproduced with the kind permission of the Chief Constable of Thames Valley Police, the successors to Buckinghamshire Police.

Alan Davis (PC50) – Bucks Constabulary and Thames Valley Police – 1959–1990

In 1963 I was the village bobby in the small village of Stewkley, situated in Buckinghamshire close to the Bedfordshire border. I patrolled about five other villages on my 250cc Triumph motorcycle which had all round grey faring. My motor cycling kit – helmet, goggles and jacket – were identical to those shown in the TV series *Heartbeat*. For me it was an idyllic life where the village bobby was on a par with the vicar and well respected by all.

On Thursday 8 August 1963 the Great Train Robbery took place at Bridego Railway Bridge at Ledburn near Mentmore. This was on an adjoining 'beat', patrolled by Police Constable Derek Bennett who was stationed at Cheddington. It was, at that time, the crime of the century. We as constables were far too lowly to be part of the investigation but I nevertheless went sometime later on my motorcycle to look at the scene which was only about five miles away from Stewkley.

I can recall a grey haired Detective Superintendent Fewtrell of our Buckinghamshire Constabulary being in charge of the investigation, but very quickly Detective Chief Superintendent Tommy Butler from the London Metropolitan Police led the investigation with his side-kick Detective Sergeant Jack Slipper.

Within a few days of the robbery a farm called Leatherslade Farm, between Oakley and Brill was found to be the hideout of the gang of robbers. For several days I and other Constables were detailed to guard the farm. I recall seeing the open backed lorry and Land Rover that had apparently been used by the robbers.

In January 1964 the trial took place of about a dozen or so of the robbers and others involved. It was held in a large room in the offices of Aylesbury Rural District Council which at that time was in Walton Street, Aylesbury. Together with a number of other Constables, I was given the job of guarding the prisoners as they arrived in a prison van from Aylesbury Prison.

Inspector Jackson was in charge of us and barked out his orders as we handcuffed one prisoner to ourselves before they alighted from the van. To me as a young bobby, Inspector Jackson was an intimidating character, perhaps an ex-military man. We then took the prisoners into the court and sat in a specially constructed dock which held all the prisoners and their constable guards. I can recall being fascinated by how smart the prisoners were; most in suit, shirt and tie. I can recall Ronald Biggs, Bruce Reynolds (a big burly man), and Charlie Wilson who looked like a London spiv, James Hussey a rather quiet man and Douglas Gordon Goody who was about six feet tall and often dressed in a roll neck pullover and sports jacket. I also recall lesser mortals like Roger Cordrey and Brian Field, the solicitor's clerk who helped the robbers in finding Leatherslade farm. The trial went on until April when sentencing took place. I think everyone was shocked by the thirty-year prison sentences handed out.

My last recollection is being handcuffed to James White in April 1966 after he was arrested for his part in the robbery. Somewhere there is a photograph of me in my motorcycling jacket handcuffed to him.

Brian Wood (PC160 & 306) – Bucks Constabulary and Thames Valley Police – 1955–1986

It was at 6am on the morning of Thursday 8 August 1963 that I was awoken from my slumber by someone knocking loudly on the door of my house. It was my traffic sergeant. He told me that a train had been robbed on my beat and over a million pounds stolen. The Great Train Robbery had just taken place and I was required to report for duty.

For the next few months my colleagues and I in the Traffic Department were glorified chauffeurs in our Jaguar patrol cars for the senior CID officers of the Buckinghamshire Constabulary and the Metropolitan Police investigating the crime.

The police operation was highly successful and it is believed that only two of the original gang escaped prosecution by fleeing overseas. Of the £2,631,684 stolen (equivalent to £41,000,000 today), about three-quarters of a million pounds was recovered.

Our tasks were to pick up the prisoners as and when they were arrested and take them to Aylesbury Police Station, transporting exhibits and carrying out any other such duties. It was quite a hectic few months.

After the discovery of the robber's lair at Leatherslade Farm, an incident room was set up at Brill Police Station where I worked for a short time in the incident room, mainly manning the switchboard and dealing with callers.

When the trial started on 20 January 1964 at Aylesbury Assizes under Mr Justice Edmund Davis, my colleague and I escorted the fifteen prisoners to and from Aylesbury prison to the specially converted courthouse twice a day. This duty continued for the duration of the fifty-one day trial.

During this time my colleagues and I got to know all of the robbers quite well. Some members of the public and the press may have expressed a grudging admiration of the robbers for their audacity in executing the robbery; however, we knew them as a bunch of vicious, unscrupulous thugs who deserved the heavy penalties imposed on them.

Of the fifteen arrested, eleven were convicted of a number of criminal offences and sent to prison for between three and thirty years.

Initially, the money recovered by the police was placed in a safe in the Chief Constable's office but he later decided the money should be put in a more secure location. Therefore, my colleague and I were entrusted to take this huge amount of money to the Bank of England in Threadneedle Street, London.

We used a prison van loaned from the Metropolitan Police and a dog handler with his Alsatian sat in the back of the van with the money. We set off for London and as we approached the City my colleague and I discussed whether we should continue on or by-pass London, catch the ferry to France and proceed to Spain where the booty would provide us with a good living. It was all a joke of course; we would not lower ourselves to the level of the robbers.

The 8 August 1963 was due to be the Bucks Constabulary sports day and I was scheduled to run in the one mile race. This was of course cancelled which was a blessing as I had not been training!

At a meeting of the Buckinghamshire Constabulary Association in April 2012, I spoke with several of my colleagues about years gone by and we could only think of three or four of the officers who were actively engaged in the Great Train Robbery and were still with us, time has taken its toll.

John Pearson (PC585) – Bucks Constabulary and Thames Valley Police – 1958–1988

My association with the Great Train Robbery is limited, for I was early in my service and I was stationed at Gerrards Cross.

The trial was not held in the old 'Assize' (Crown Court) building located in the main square in Aylesbury but at the Council Offices down the road near to Aylesbury Police Station itself, as the facilities were bigger and better there.

My duties for the day in question were to carry out traffic duty outside the court entrance across a busy main road. I made myself extremely unpopular with a senior officer attending the trial, when I waived in a smart Jaguar (one of the gang's wives I soon discovered) in preference to him. You can't win them all!

My experience with the senior officer made it one of my 'off days' in that he decided to tell me off in front of the public. However, the following day down at Fulmer I pursued a burglar across field and wood for several miles before I caught up with him, disarmed him of his large jemmy and arrested him. A much better day altogether!

When the trial was in progress my job was to guard the prisoners in the courtroom itself along with other officers. We were not armed nor, as I recall it, particularly well briefed but fortunately security was never actually a problem throughout the proceedings as far as I know.

When the news came in that morning (when I was on early turn shift) our general comments were about the amount actually stolen by the gang and national inflation. We considered it perhaps would have been a better idea to have nicked the train itself as it was probably worth more at the time!

Keith Milner (PC540) – Bucks Constabulary and Thames Valley Police – 1956–1987

I was one of five Detective Constables based at Aylesbury and had to be home by 2am on Wednesday 8 August 1963, as from that time I was the on call CID cover for the division. I climbed into bed just prior to 2am and was 'called out' by the Bucks HQ Information Room sometime around 5am.

Such a call was not an unusual occurrence, but what was said was different. 'There's been a burglary at Cheddington Railway Station,' the caller said. 'What's gone?' I said. 'A train,' was the reply. I quickly washed, shaved and dressed in suit, collar and tie. An early call out was generally the precursor to a long day – and this was to be no exception.

After collecting my fingerprint searcher's kit and a bundle of statement forms I drove to Cheddington Station where a scene of some confusion was evident. This is not unusual at the scene of a major crime but by resorting to routine practices and procedures some sort of order is eventually restored. I did some fingerprint searching at a ganger's hut which had been broken into and then began to take statements from some of the post office staff.

I was soon interrupted by Detective Superintendent Fewtrell, the Head of Bucks CID, and told to 'go up the track, collect, identify, label and record any material evidence connected to the robbery.' That order committed me to the GTR enquiry for the next nine months and irretrievably for the rest of my service.

On the track I began to realise the enormity of the crime and the intense press interest. Around 9am a reporter from *The London Evening News* approached me and asked if I could confirm that a million pounds had been stolen. Such speculation amazed me and I told him that I had no idea. My photograph, in splendid and distant isolation on the fast track, appeared on the front page of the paper that evening – the first and only time I have achieved such prominence.

Throughout the morning I was aware of the numerous light aircraft constantly circulating the scene – no helicopters – just light aircraft. Fleet Street was present in force. That was the case throughout the enquiry and ever afterwards.

I returned to Cheddington Station around 12pm where I saw Phil Fairweather, my Detective Sergeant. Neither of us had eaten or even had a 'cuppa' since being called out. There was nothing at the Railway Station but we found a nearby pub which served only a pint of bitter and the worst hamburger I have ever tasted. Before we had finished, senior officers summoned us for a 'consolidation meeting', prior to their departure to New Scotland Yard (NSY), for a conference to determine the way forward. I continued with my task of collating and recording exhibits which eventually, in the months to come, reached a total nearing 2,000.

The following day the enquiry was headed by Detective Supt Gerald McArthur from NSY, assisted by his Sergeant Jack Pritchard. Malcolm Fewtrell was designated second in charge and the enquiry really got underway. The rest is history, the discovery of Leatherslade Farm, the arrests in Bournemouth and then in London and around.

Bucks Police HQ in Walton Grove, Aylesbury became the centre of a huge crime investigation, perhaps one of the largest ever undertaken. As the Exhibits Officer I accumulated a considerable knowledge of the investigation and was able to contribute on occasions. The Flying Squad were heavily involved from the outset and we had a good liaison with them.

I was very impressed with the Squad's head, Detective Chief Superintendent Tommy Butler, who was very good to me and helped me over the years. Some of my associations with his team lasted throughout my career and included Jim Nevill who ended his service as head of the Anti-Terrorist Squad, and Nipper Read who dealt with the Krays.

The GTR is now a part of British folklore and I will always remember the total commitment of those involved in the investigation.

The trial began in a specially constructed courtroom in the Aylesbury Rural District Council Offices on 20 January 1964. Twenty people were accused in connection with the crime. At the outset the lead prosecuting counsel, Arthur James QC, asked Judge Edmund Davies (who later headed the Royal Commission into the Police Service) if I could remain in court throughout the proceedings. This was agreed and I was present in court for the whole of the trial until its conclusion on 23 March (the 48th day). With the assistance of Bill Cullen, I had prepared over 1,000 exhibits for court production and actually produced 613. My evidence and thorough cross examination lasted for the best part of a day. There were four barristers for the prosecution and twenty-seven for the defence, including ten QCs.

The trial had its own dramas which included: a Detective Inspector's mistake leading to Bigg's retrial; and Daly being acquitted against all the odds on the 20th day and a juror reporting a bribery attempt. There were moments of humour and tension. The Counsel for Welch carelessly cross examined a witness and the answers he received clearly implicated his client. When Counsel sat down Welch leaned forward and whispered just one word: 'c**t'. That word was heard by everyone and no doubt helped to convict him. A moment which caused a rare outbreak of laughter was when a neighbour of Leatherslade Farm was asked by a rather supercilious Counsel, 'When you go to Leatherslade Farm do you ascend a gradient?' His rather confused and agitated reply was, 'No, I always goes up the 'ill'

The Judge's summing up began on the 42nd day and finished six days later on 23 March. The Jury returned at 8.05pm two days later, finding all guilty on at least one count. Biggs' trial began on 8 April and all were sentenced on 16 April at the old Assize Court in Market Square, Aylesbury.

The judges' address to Brigadier Cheney the Chief Constable at the trial's conclusion was very complimentary to the police and he named and commended a number of officers individually.

I have long held the view that the initial manpower difficulties encountered and the general logistics involved may well have influenced the formation of the Regional Crime Squads and even force amalgamations later in the decade.

Leonard Woodley (PC560) – Bucks Constabulary & TVP – 1959–1989

I was a uniform constable at Aylesbury at the time of the Great Train Robbery.

On Saturday 10 August 1963, I was due to go on early turn shift, i.e. 6am to 2pm. I was called out early, told to take my sandwiches with me and I was taken to Cheddington Railway siding where I was placed at a gate and told to guard the attacked coaches that had been placed there. I was not to let anyone near the coaches until the investigating detectives arrived at the scene later that morning.

It was a fine day and for a while I had the whole place to myself. Then the press reporters, some of whom were staying at the nearby hotel overlooking the siding, came and asked me if they could approach the coaches to have a look round and to take photographs of them. I said that they were not permitted any closer than the gate where I was standing and they would have to wait and speak to the senior officers when they arrived. They accepted this, and then asked if they returned to the hotel, could they take some photographs of me walking up and down the track by the coaches so that they could take photographs of me guarding the scene of the crime. I couldn't see any harm in that and told them that that would be alright with me as long as they were quick and finished before any officers arrived. So, whilst they scuttled off back to the hotel, I passed through the gate and duly walked up and down the track looking very important as they clicked away.

A few minutes later I was joined at the scene by PC Jim Adams, now deceased, and we kept watch until the detectives, photographers and fingerprint officers arrived. Now I never saw any photographs or films of me walking up and down the track but whenever there is something about the robbery shown on television, there is Jim Adams and I, standing by the gate.

When the robbers' hideaway was discovered at Leatherslade Farm some days later, I was detailed to guard these premises with another policeman (can't remember who). One of us was to stay in the farm whilst the other stood down by the gate at the entrance to the farm. We were given walkie-talkie radios so that we could keep in touch with each other. Now the gate at the entrance and the farm were only a few yards apart but the radios we had were absolutely useless! We could not contact each other and it was a blessing when dawn came so that we could see each other and wave.

When the robbers were captured and committed for trial, which was held at the old Aylesbury Rural District Council Offices in Walton Street, Aylesbury, there was a big police presence either handcuffed to each robber or manning the traffic points to enable the prison vans to get from Aylesbury Prison to the council offices without a hold up. One day, I was handcuffed to a robber whilst he was in transition and un-handcuffed at the offices to await entry into the court-room. In those days, during the daylight hours, we were required to wear white gloves and one policeman had left his on a chair at the offices. One of the robbers, Wisbey I think, saw them, picked them up, put them on and did a little song and dance routine for the entertainment of the police and his fellow robbers. It helped to lighten the tension.

The robbers were found guilty and it was decided that they would be sentenced, not at the Rural District Council Offices, but at the old Assize Court, as it was then, in Market Square, Aylesbury. I happened to be off duty that day, so I went along to the court building and managed to get in right by the prisoner's dock.

The judge and all the officials came in to the court and the first prisoner was put up to be sentenced (they did not appear all at once). He came up the steps from the cells below and the judge told him that he would be sentenced to thirty years imprisonment. Someone in the public gallery cried out, 'Oh!' Never ever had a sentence of such length been passed before. I forget who the prisoner was but as he turned and went back down the steps he cried out, 'Don't worry, I can do it'.

Michael Eyles (PC237) – Bucks Constabulary & Thames Valley Police – 1961–1991

I joined the Buckinghamshire Constabulary on the 13th February 1961 and I remember hearing about the Great Train Robbery when I received a telephone call from a colleague at Beaconsfield Police Station.

I was making a conference point, stood outside the telephone kiosk at Old Beaconsfield roundabout, in the days before radios and mobile phones. It all sounded very exciting particularly as my home was in Bletchley before joining up, and I knew the location of Bridego Bridge fairly well. Little did I know that I was going to be called upon to take some minor active part in what followed.

Scenes of Crime were gathering evidence. I was only there for one day but it was an occasion that I would never forget. We were shown round the scene and I can remember seeing the vehicles in the outbuildings, which looked like army lorries. I can remember there was a lot of activity that day with coming and going from the farmhouse itself, but my tour of duty passed off without incident.

Some months later I was drafted in to Aylesbury when the trial of the Great Train Robbery commenced at specially converted council offices which had been turned into a court for the occasion. The role of junior officers was to be handcuffed to the individuals whilst they were waiting to go into the court and to sit with them whilst they were sat in the dock. We were warned not to have any discussion with them whatsoever and I believe they were told not to communicate with us either.

I was surprised that there was no friction between us and them and most of them seemed to have quite a good sense of humour.

I was only engaged in this operation for one, possibly two days and I can remember being very careful not to say anything of any significance, to make sure that I didn't drop a clanger. However it was impossible to sit handcuffed to these people all day without any conversation at all, particularly whilst waiting to go into the court. I can remember that there was a bit of banter between us all, when they attempted to take the mickey out of the country bumpkin coppers but they were very quickly reminded that it was them that were on trial and not us.

Years later I remember visiting Aylesbury Prison on a totally unrelated matter, which happened to be the prison where they were remanded whilst the trial was on-going. I was told that they came very close to making an escape attempt from the prison, which was thwarted when partially completed skeleton keys were seized.

CHAPTER FIVE

The Conditions

(More new stuff about the politics that pushed the investigation)

After every war there is an epidemic of crime. Men sent away to fight a war return home, confused, troubled and trained in violence. After the First World War, the Assistant Commissioner in charge of the Criminal Investigation Department (CID) at New Scotland Yard, Sir Basil Thompson, faced this dilemma. He was also aware that his detectives were hampered in their efforts by a lack of transport and strict rules that required them to secure the personal approval of an officer of the rank of Superintendent in order to cross over a divisional boundary for any reason. Clearly, there was a need to make his officers 'more fluid'.

His solution was to summon two of his best thief-takers, Chief Inspector Frederick Porter Wensley and Inspector Walter Hambrook and instruct them to select the twelve best detectives in the Metropolitan Police to form a new squad which would be allowed to travel all over the Metropolitan Police District, and beyond if necessary, in order to investigate crimes and pursue criminals.

Scotland Yard has had three incarnations in its one hundred and seventy-five year history, with a fourth scheduled for 2015. Originally situated at 4 Whitehall Place with a rear entrance on Great Scotland Yard, in 1890 it moved to the Norman Shaw Buildings on Victoria Embankment, overlooking the River Thames, in buildings that now provide offices and other facilities for Members of Parliament. However, the requirements of modern technology and further increases in the size of the force meant that by 1967 it had outgrown this site and New Scotland Yard moved to the present building situated at the junction of Broadway and Victoria Street. In May 2013 the Metropolitan Police confirmed that the current New Scotland Yard building will be sold and the force's headquarters will be moved to the Curtis Green Building on the Victoria Embankment, which will be renamed 'Scotland Yard'.

In October 1918 a meeting of the selected detectives was held in an office on the second floor of the Norman Shaw Building. The officers were addressed by Chief Inspector Frederick Porter Wensley and Inspector Walter Hambrook, who told them of their plans for the new unit.

Initially, the squad was provided with a horse-drawn covered wagon hired, appropriately, from the Great Western Railway. Criminals were frequently surprised to be arrested by detectives who 'came out of nowhere'. It took several months before the underworld started to realise that these detectives were using a covered wagon with holes cut in the side to observe their activities.

After two years, in 1920, the squad was supplied with two Crossley Motor Tenders that had become surplus to the requirements of the Royal Flying Corps at the end of the war. The tenders were capable of reaching 40 mph but were not fitted with front brakes and had narrow tyres, which made them difficult to handle at speed or in the wet. This was the first time that police had been equipped with motor vehicles and the news was released to the press. W.G.T. Crook, crime reporter for *The Daily Mail* christened the squad, 'The Flying Squad'. Edgar Wallace wrote a book and a play of the same title and it quickly caught the public's imagination and stuck. As the tenders could each hold ten men, the size of the squad was increased to twenty officers.

Few people owned a motor vehicle at this time. The Commissioner of the Metropolitan Police, Sir Edward Henry, is believed to have been the first police officer in the country to have purchased a motor vehicle when he bought one in 1907 that he also used at work. With little changing between 1914 and 1918, as most people went off to fight in the First World War, this meant that in 1920 the best drivers were those who had been trained in the services during the war.

It soon became clear that a major problem with the tenders was the inability to keep in touch with Scotland Yard, so that they could be directed to the scenes of crimes or alerted to the sightings of suspects, so experiments in wireless telephony and telegraphy started in 1921. Problems encountered included losing the signal in built-up areas, and interference from telegraph wires, steel bridges, trams and other motor vehicles. Eventually an aerial consisting of two adjustable arms with five wires slung between them was found to be effective, but had the disadvantage of attracting the attention of the criminals who called the modified vehicles 'bedsteads'.

Initially telegraphy was found superior to telephony and a number of former Royal Navy radio operators, skilled in Morse code, were identified and five of them were recruited to set up the first Information Room at New Scotland Yard, with others who could maintain high speeds of transmission during high-speed pursuits posted to work on the tenders.

The new Flying Squad had an immediate effect on crime and criminals. Fred Wensley was not the sort of 'guv'nor' to hide in his office and deal with paperwork and he frequently accompanied his officers on patrol, particularly when violence was anticipated or villains were to be arrested. Sixteen hour days quickly became the norm.

Wensley recognised the importance of police officers being well informed and, coming from the East End of London, he encouraged his officers to frequent the inns and taverns where criminals could be found and to build links with potential informants.

Over the next half century the Flying Squad established itself as an essential element in controlling crime in London. The number of officers and the number, quality and range of vehicles available to the squad had improved. The squad drivers were now the finest graduates of the Metropolitan Police Motor Driving School at Hendon, and employed the principles of driving technique set down in the 'Roadcraft' book. The radios in the squad vehicles were now reliant on telephony and were entrusted to the detectives themselves rather than to specialist radio operators.

In this way, the Flying Squad were capable of fighting crime in whatever form it took and wherever it occurred. They were able to pursue and detain those on the road, confront and restrain large, violent gangs of pickpockets on the racecourses, and use firearms to confront and overwhelm armed robbers in the act of robbing banks and building societies. They worked hard, played hard and generally got their man.

In 1963, the Flying Squad was a team of around 100 detectives, based at New Scotland Yard, which at that time still occupied the Norman Shaw Building on the Embankment, near the Houses of Parliament on the north side of the River Thames. The Flying Squad office was on the fourth floor, with one wall lined with the offices of the senior squad officers, and another wall with a row of telephone cubicles where officers could take calls from confidential informants about armed robberies and other major crimes; crimes that if the perpetrators ever suspected that they had been discussed with the police would cost the informants their lives. All the officers selected by Tommy Butler to investigate the Great Train Robbery worked in this office, but for the duration of the enquiry they moved their desks to one corner of the office so as to be able to work together.

Chiefs of the Flying Squad from Fred Wensley to Tommy Butler all worked exceptionally long hours at the Yard, even when there was nothing special happening, so when there was a 'big job' on, they would have worked very long hours and expected their men to do likewise. CID officers worked either Early Turn (E/T) or Late Turn (L/T) with a week on Night Duty (N/D) when working on Division. Early Turn was the normal office hours of 9 am to 5 pm but no senior officer would be happy to see his men go home before 7 pm or 8 pm. Late Turn was 2 pm to 10 pm with nobody leaving much before midnight.

Butler made it clear to his officers that he would produce a roster showing them E/T or L/T, but that he would expect everybody to be at work by 9 am and that he would not expect them to leave until they had worked sixteen hours, at 1 am the next day. Frank Williams related the story of a day when he and Butler were out chasing suspects all night and returned to the Yard at 8.45 am. Williams, exhausted, turned left to go home, but was recalled by Butler who pointed out that the next shift started in fifteen minutes and that he would be late for it if he was not careful.

As detectives, the squad all received Detective Duty Allowance (DDA) which, as well as being compensation for not being paid for the overtime that they were frequently required to do, was also supposed to cover the purchase and cleaning of the clothes that they wore at work, which would vary from suits, shirts and ties for court, maybe blazer and flannels, shirts and ties for office work and more casual clothing for surveillance work or if they anticipated serious violence. In truth, the money did not cover the weekly tea club bill.

The life of a detective during a major enquiry would not please his or her doctor. Very long hours of work, restricted opportunities for sleep, missed meals, snatched meals, plenty of stress, and an almost complete lack of exercise can seriously affect your health and it must have come as only a slight shock when Jack Slipper suffered with an outbreak of boils all over his body during the enquiry into the Great Train Robbery.

Plain clothes officers in the Metropolitan Police are not generally permitted to work alone, due to the nature and range of allegations that may be made against them. Although there is a recognition that CID officers may have to work alone on certain enquiries, every effort is made to avoid this where possible. Accordingly the six officers on the 'Special Enquiry Team' selected by Tommy Butler to investigate the Great Train Robbery were divided into three pairs:

Detective Inspector Frank Williams
Detective Sergeant Stanley (Steve) Moore
Detective Sergeant Jack Slipper
Detective Sergeant Jim Nevill
Detective Sergeant Lou van Dyck
Detective Constable Tommy Thorburn.

The statement that this team was the best of the best, a squad chosen by Tommy Butler from the best of the detectives on the Metropolitan Police Flying Squad, who were themselves the best detectives in the Metropolitan Police, is supported by the fact that five of these six officers had achieved the rank of Detective Chief Superintendent by the time that they retired, and that Jim Nevill was the Commander of the Anti-Terrorist Branch.

Each pair of officers would have the use of a Flying Squad car and driver whenever they needed it, to go wherever they needed to go.

The Metropolitan Police is very fortunate to be extremely well served by the Metropolitan Police Catering Service, which runs refectories at all offices, stations and at every major incident or major crime scene and which can provide all day breakfasts, sandwiches and drinks as well as a range of popular meals. The squad would have been able to rely on these facilities at New Scotland Yard twenty-four hours a day.

Whilst uniformed police officers are subject to constant supervision by their supervisors, only disappearing for a few minutes at a time to investigate a crime and then report back, the supervision of detectives who need to move around in plain clothes, perform surveillance duties, make discreet enquiries into sexual crimes, meet confidential informants in public houses, etc., is more difficult, and the system that has been designed includes two time management systems, duty states and diaries.

Duty states sit in a prominent position in the CID Office, where they may be inspected by any police or civilian member of staff with access to the private areas of a police station, to establish the location of a CID officer who may be urgently required at court or by a senior officer. The state contains a sheet for every officer based in the office and is completed by the officer concerned, in advance, so that if he or she leaves the office in order to search an address, they record this on the duty state. If, on the way to the address, they arrest three men committing an armed robbery, then at the first opportunity they must update the state with the fact that they made the arrests and are now engaged with the prisoners at some police station. This, of course, means that the state is frequently incorrect as events have overtaken the planned activities.

Diaries are hard-bound books held by the officer, usually under lock and key in his or her desk. It should be brought up to date two or three times a day and should be a historical record of what actually happened as well as justifying any overtime or expenses claimed by the officer. The officer may be required to instantly produce the diary at any time in order that his supervisors may check his activities and ensure that it is up-to-date.

Diaries and duty states are frequently required to be produced at court so that defence barristers may compare the duty states and diaries with the note books, and discrepancies between the three documents identified. Anybody who believes that an inconsistency between any of these documents is evidence of wrongdoing should attempt to record their day's work in three separate ways and then invite a friend to compare them. It is almost impossible, even if you are not working sixteen hour action-packed days with many other responsibilities. In fact, the fact that all three documents are consistent is the best possible evidence of corruption as it is almost impossible when attempted by an honest person.

All these documents must be checked and signed weekly by the officer's supervisors, so that any overtime and expenses claims can be checked and any inconsistencies identified. In addition, the duty states will be checked and initialled periodically throughout each day and diaries once or twice each week. Note books are signed by the Custody Officer dealing with each prisoner as soon as possible after the arrest and no later than at the time of charging.

Although the Great Train Robbery occurred too late for it to appear in the morning papers, there can be little doubt that news of the robbery met every government minister and most chief executives of national bodies, by the time that they arrived at work at 9 am. Calls must have been flying around Whitehall between ministers and across London between representatives of the Post Office, British Rail, Buckinghamshire Constabulary, the British Transport Police, the Post Office Investigations Branch and all the major banks, as people tried to come to terms with what had happened and the consequences of what happened.

Most of the banks had not been insured against their losses and their only hope of recovering the stolen money lay in the arrest of the culprits and the recovery of the money by the police. The pride and reputation of the other public bodies involved in the robbery would have motivated them to secure an early and complete result to the enquiry. The Prime Minister called the Home Secretary expressing his desire for firm and decisive police action and promising the support needed by the

Home Secretary in order to achieve this. All this would have culminated in extreme pressure being applied by the Home Office for a quick and decisive result.

This pressure manifested itself in the transfer of responsibility for the enquiry being passed from Buckinghamshire Constabulary to the Metropolitan Police. It then extended to the allocation of resources and the setting of priorities, so that officers would know that any ambitions that they held would be affected by their performance and success on the enquiry.

The only other crime in recent English criminal history, in which a similar pressure was brought to bear by politicians on police officers to solve a crime, was the Yorkshire Ripper Enquiry, when nineteen women were killed. On that occasion, the pressure on senior officers to resolve the case led to them throwing resources of every kind into the enquiry, ranging from detectives, uniformed officers, forensic scientists, administrators, cars, motorcycles, offices, computers, etc. and the sheer quantity of information held by the enquiry team filled entire police stations until nobody could find anything any longer and the suspect was eventually arrested by almost the only two officers in West Yorkshire Police NOT engaged on the enquiry wandering onto a murder and arresting the suspect, Peter Sutcliffe by good old-fashioned uniformed policing.

Unlike in the United States of America, where many investigations are affected by political interference either to pressure detectives to solve a crime or to desist from investigating a crime, there is almost no political pressure brought to bear on the British Police. The foundations of the British Police were set down by Sir Robert Peel and elaborated by the first two Commissioners of the Metropolitan Police, Sir Richard Mayne and Sir Charles Rowan, who felt that each officer should be an independent Crown Appointment, personally responsible for the execution of his duties. Since Margaret Thatcher's time as Prime Minister this has evolved so that senior officers have more corporate responsibility, and politicians interfere in policing, which has weakened both the strength and integrity of the system.

Chapter Six

The Investigation

(This is a critical and theoretical analysis of the process of investigating the crime...More new stuff)

Introduction

Armed robbery is a special crime and is committed by the 'Princes of the Underworld'. This is not to be read as showing anything other than the grudging respect due to a worthy opponent. It is committed by well-armed and extremely violent men who must be prepared to kill every time that they go to work. A person who takes a gun, knife or other deadly weapon out of the house must be prepared to use it, or expect it to be used by others, to kill him. Women seldom display the sheer violence and aggression necessary to commit this crime.

Men who commit armed robbery are usually big, strong, shrewd, clever, well-organised, confident and brave because nobody wins every fight, however strong or well-armed they are. However, most of them are still unable to go to work without the benefit of drugs and/or alcohol to steady their nerves.

Of course, being big, strong, confident and carrying a wad of cash will make robbers into 'faces', well known men in their community. The fact that they regularly require the assistance of their colleagues in the underworld and that they have the ready cash necessary to pay for these services, also makes them popular.

An average armed robbery will frequently require:

- somebody to supply firearms
- somebody to dispose of firearms
- somebody to supply getaway cars
- somebody to dispose of getaway cars

- other robbers to assist him
- getaway drivers
- men with inside knowledge of potential crimes
- somebody who they can trust to look after the loot

On my first day as an operational police officer, I was sent to Carter Street Police Station in Walworth, near the Elephant and Castle in South London. There I was met by Superintendent (later Chief Superintendent) Gordon Thomson, the Deputy Divisional Commander and until that time a lecturer at Bramshill Police College. Mr Thomson gave a lecture on crime in which he explained the origins of armed robbery in London:

'In centuries gone by, Londinium was a walled city, with gates to the north of the city, in Islington, and to the south of the city, at London Bridge and these gates were protected by guards who restricted entry to the city. Those outside the city believed the streets of the city to be paved with gold and the rogues and vagabonds kept trying to get into the city and kept being prevented from doing so by these guards. The rogues and vagabonds then waited outside the gates to the city for another chance to try to enter, so they formed communities outside the gates which evolved into the criminal underworld. In South London the underworld set up in Bermondsey and Rotherhithe and ninety-five per cent of the armed robbers in England were based there.'

The Metropolitan Police has responded to the threat posed by armed robbers by sending in the 'Flying Squad', 'C8', 'the Sweeney', 'the Heavy Mob', 'the Commissioner's Private Army'. For (almost) the last one hundred years the best, the brightest, and the most ambitious young detectives in London have aspired not to a career in the Murder Squad, the Regional Crime Squad or the Serious Crimes Squad, but to a career in the Flying Squad.

The Flying Squad is tasked only with investigating armed robbery, whether it be in banks, building societies, post offices, betting shops, casinos, or wherever. It does this by studying armed robberies and armed robbers from all over the United

Kingdom, and all over the world, so that it is able to identify and predict patterns of crime. The detectives are expected to visit the public houses and clubs which suspects frequent, and to develop confidential informants in order to gather information about active robbers and future crimes. The detectives and the robbers very quickly get to know each other.

The Metropolitan Police Flying Squad works in a different way than any other force of detectives in the United Kingdom, possibly in the world. Usually crimes are reported to the Police by members of the public who are the victims of those crimes. "I have been robbed", "He raped me" and so on. These allegations are then documented and detectives are delegated to investigate the allegations. In the words of Gil Grissom, the central character in the American television drama *CSI*, 'Follow the evidence' and then arrest the person at the end of the trail. Extensive records are kept at the Police Station of all enquiries, so that if a detective becomes ill or injured, or dies, other detectives may take up the investigation, without any noticeable delay or disruption to the enquiry.

The Flying Squad is made up of the best detectives. They are given the biggest and best cars in town. If four very large men are going to 'live' in the car for days on end, taking it in turns to eat, drink and sleep whilst keeping suspects under surveillance, then chase down armed robbers who have stolen the best cars available and hired racing drivers who can regularly beat Formula 1 World Champions, in the way that Roy James did in the 1960s, in order to avoid 30 year prison sentences, then the cars and the drivers have to be the best available. Flying Squad officers do not themselves drive. They have always had racing drivers to drive them around in racing cars. They call the ramp outside New Scotland Yard 'The Flight Deck'. An urgent call will result in a quick call to the Drivers' Office, 'Bring the car up onto the Flight Deck and I will meet you there.'

Flying Squad detectives frequently wait outside public houses for them to open and stay there until they close, several hours after the end of formal licensing hours. Many of the South London 'boozers' frequented by DI Frank Williams in the 1960s would have served an excellent 'big-boy's' breakfast at around 8 am, (to those who had been locked-in all night) just in time to settle the detective's stomach to give evidence at the Old Bailey at 10 am.

These detectives sit there drinking beer and whisky, greeting the most dangerous and violent criminals in the country to discuss items of mutual interest, like crime. Outwardly innocent conversations, such as 'I haven't seen Fred recently' can mean 'Is Fred planning a big job or in prison after a big job?' and 'I see that Fred's in the money this week,' can mean 'What crime has Fred committed recently?' and so on.

Payments for information

Men appearing regularly at the Old Bailey need friends and frequently need help. Brief facts supplied to the court after a guilty plea can be brief or go into lurid detail. In the 1960s and 1970s the Criminal Record Office (CRO) was allowed to fall behind in its record keeping. Lists of convictions supplied to the court could be complete and up-to-date, or one or two of the most serious convictions could be 'forgotten'. People who were short of money could always tell stories to the detectives in exchange for cash.

On the day that the Great Train Robbery occurred, Frank Williams was immediately able to name the gang involved and was pretty accurate with his list of suspects. He had known that they were active, that they had conducted the armed robbery at the offices of BOAC at Comet House, and that they had been conducting scouting operations on motorcycles around Cheddington where the robbery took place. He had even made a point of meeting up with Bruce Reynolds and letting him know that he was being watched.

Detectives record their expenses in their diaries. These include bus and train tickets, the occasional taxi ride, meals wasted due to unexpected overtime. Then there are the 'incidental expenses' for intoxicating liquor in public houses to secure information on crime. Detectives posted to local police stations get around £10-£15 for three pints of beer or so. Flying Squad officers get substantially more. In 1984 I was posted to the Anti-Terrorist Branch. I was involved in the investigation of the Harrods Bomb, where I got the job of sweeping up the body of Police Sergeant Noel Lane, who had sat next to me at school for six years.

Commander Bill Hucklesby authorised up to £1,000 per week in 'incidental expenses' to each of the 200 officers involved, for several months after. The Deputy Commissioner over-ruled this decision, but was himself over-ruled by the Commissioner, who recognised the need for investment in order to secure results.

The Metropolitan Police Fund will authorise payments of a few hundred pounds to those who supply useful information to detectives and who meet certain criteria. Accurate records must be kept, but access to these records is very strictly limited.

However, the biggest 'reward' money comes from Insurance Companies who have insured against a Theft or Damage and are keen to catch those responsible and deter repeat offences. These payments (generally ten per cent of the sum stolen) are usually recommended by detectives and approved by the insurer's loss adjusters, often retired detectives making good use of their skills, and usually personally paid out by very senior detectives, so as to ensure propriety and eliminate unjustified allegations against junior detectives.

Trust and confidentiality are essential. An armed robber arrested 'crossing the pavement' waving a sawn-off shotgun at a security guard and confronted by a team of armed Flying Squad detectives, may have anything up to 30 years sitting in a prison cell, trying to work out who 'grassed him up', deciding on a suitable penalty, which can be anything from maiming to death, and working out how to arrange it and pay for it without being detected and sentenced to further imprisonment.

The Flying Squad system requires the senior managers to trust their officers, who are out of the office, sitting in pubs or fast cars, meeting with the most dangerous criminals in the country and frequently drinking more than they should. That would be enough to give most managers apoplexy! The Flying Squad detectives are assessed by their results; the number of 'serious faces' that they lock up in the year. They are expected to pick up a few complaints over the year, but nobody worries too much about them.

An Overview

The popular view states that the Great Train Robbery was committed by a gang of clowns, who eventually got their just desserts, and were duly tracked down, arrested, convicted and sentenced to very long prison sentences. However, Detective Inspector Frank Williams, who managed the investigation, under the supervision and tactical direction of his superior, Detective Chief Superintendent Tommy Butler, stated in his autobiographical book *No Fixed Address* that the Great Train Robbery was committed 'by a highly-trained and well-disciplined gang of men' and that the enquiry had to work hard in order to achieve 'the limited degree of success it attained.' He then went on to explain the reasoning behind his view was that, 'At least three men who were directly involved are still at liberty and enjoying to the full extent their share of the stolen money.' So which version is correct?

The Great Train Robbery was exceptionally well conceived, planned and executed, although as with most activities managed by a committee, errors were made when one or two things inevitably went wrong during the execution of the robbery and adjustments had to be made to the plan. This is demonstrated by the fact that when the old man recruited by Ronnie Biggs to move the train was unable to do so they forced the original driver Jack Mills to move it but they allowed him to see the vehicles that they had disguised as military vehicles, so that he reported this to the Police and, as a consequence, the gang were later unable to use the vehicles to leave the farm as they had originally planned. Also, after they had left the farm, the committee failed to monitor that the clean-up that they had commissioned and paid for had been successfully carried out so that the robbers were safe from arrest as a result of their fingerprints being found at the farm. Bruce Reynolds revelled in the nickname of 'The Colonel' but an autocratic army officer would have acted swiftly to resolve these issues and only a committee would have allowed these issues to drift in the way that the robbers did.

Frank Williams felt that three robbers escaped justice and that is best assessed by the fact that Roger Cordrey who was arrested just four days after the robbery was found in possession of £141,000 in cash and that he is very likely to have spent some money celebrating his success, so that the shares of each full member of the gang was around £150,000. Eighteen shares of £150,000 would have meant that there was not sufficient money to afford to pay any 'drinks' to those who helped the robbers, so it is more likely that there were just seventeen robbers, fourteen of whom were brought to justice.

Williams was also very forward-thinking in believing that it was the squad's responsibility to assist the insurance loss adjustors to recover as much of the stolen money as possible, a task that did not go well with only a little under £400,000 ever being recovered.

Williams led a team of Flying Squad detectives who were among the finest in the world. He assessed their performance against the best in the world and aimed for perfection. He claimed that the squad had to work hard in order to achieve results but this is hardly surprising. Tommy Butler was the Alex Ferguson of criminal detection. He pushed his officers to work as hard as he did, to work to the limits of their bodies, in order to achieve results.

Before the Robbery

Approximately nine months before the South West Gang, led by Bruce Reynolds, committed the Great Train Robbery, they committed another robbery at the offices of British Overseas Airways Corporation (BOAC) at Comet House near Heathrow Airport. Detective Inspector (DI) Frank Williams of 5 Squad of the Metropolitan Police Flying Squad made a point of tracking down and speaking to Reynolds in a public house toilet and letting him know that he knew that he was involved in the BOAC robbery. What is known as 'putting a shot across his bows'.

Reynolds, without admitting anything, exchanged banter with Williams and finished by asking Williams to 'Pass my best wishes to Mr Butler', that is Detective Chief Superintendent (DCS) Thomas Marius Butler, operational head of the Metropolitan Police Flying Squad at that time, a man who would later be selected to lead the enquiry into the Great Train Robbery and who would spend the last five years of his life chasing down Reynolds and putting him behind bars for thirty years.

Williams continued to monitor Reynolds and his activities and to gather evidence and information about his movements, despite the fact that Reynolds did not commit any crimes during this period, devoting his time to planning his next big job, the Great Train Robbery. This meant that following the commission of the Great Train Robbery, when Williams was appointed to the Robbery Enquiry Team, he was able to report to Butler that Reynolds had spent much of the last six months touring Buckinghamshire on a motorcycle, although without motorcycles of his own, Williams had been unable to follow him as closely as he would have liked.

The relationship between detective and robber is muddied a little by Police Confidential Informants, or 'snouts' as they are known by the Police, or 'grasses' as they are known to the robbers. These men and women provide information to the Police for a wide variety of reasons, ranging from money, favours (particularly following their own arrest), righteousness, or attempting to keep a family member out of trouble.

None of this will interest an armed robber, who will often use violence or even kill a man who he suspects of betraying him to the Police. In the Great Train Robbery, Charlie Wilson, potentially the most violent man in the gang, let it be known to all and sundry at the very first planning meeting for the robbery, that he would kill anybody who 'grassed' him to the Police. It has also been alleged that he had to be forcibly restrained by several of his colleagues when Brian Field admitted to them that he had failed to get Leatherslade Farm burnt down as he had been paid to do, before the Police found it and were able to conduct a full forensic examination of the place. Wilson is said to have wanted to kill Field then and there, in front of all his friends, as an example to them and others.

Informants live in close proximity to the armed robbers. They hear 'whispers' in public houses, but they also notice when the robbers are away from home for a few days or when they are spending a lot of money. This information would have confirmed Police suspicions that the men that they were looking for were holed up near the scene of the crime, keeping their heads down and focused their attention on finding their hideaway.

Even before the investigation of the crime was allocated to the Metropolitan Police, never mind the squad set up, detectives from the Flying Squad were speaking to their informants and seeking information on the crime and possible suspects. This was their everyday work.

After the Robbery

In the hours after the Great Train Robbery, the police investigation commenced. Local officers arrived at the scene and, having ensured that it was safe to do so, secured the area from robbers and curious members of the public. Then, realising the seriousness of the crime, they summoned their senior officers to take charge. They provided first aid to those who, like train driver Jack Mills, had been assaulted or were suffering with shock.

Very quickly witnesses were questioned and the facts as they became known were circulated to local officers, across Buckinghamshire Constabulary, to surrounding forces, and the local and national press. As sufficient officers were dragged from their beds and became available at the scene, statements were taken and a picture of what had happened began to emerge. Scenes of crime officers were called so that obvious evidence could be collected and documented. Then a formal sweep of the area to find evidence began.

Detective Superintendent Malcolm Fewtrell arrived at the scene by 5.30 am. As the Head of the CID at Buckinghamshire Constabulary, he was ultimately in charge of all criminal investigations within his Force area, and in the case of a crime of this magnitude he would have been expected to take personal charge of the investigation. Before lunch, Fewtrell had reported to his Chief Constable, Brigadier Cheney, and recommended to him that the investigation be passed to the Metropolitan Police, who had the resources and expertise to deal with it. Brigadier Cheney took Fewtrell's advice and called Commander of the Met CID, George Hatherill, to seek his assistance, just as he had finished reading the report of the robbery in the first edition of *The London Evening Standard*.

By this time it was becoming clear that the investigation had three, equally important strands:

1. To identify those responsible for the conception, execution and clear-up of the robbery
2. To establish the location of each of the suspects in order that they may be arrested at an appropriate time
3. To secure the evidence necessary to support convictions at court

By the time that the crime was reported to the Police, the suspects had decamped and the Police were left to seek information from the public on sightings or possible hideouts. The Police also organised a structured search of an area within thirty miles of the scene of the crime, working out from the scene to the perimeter. This covered Objective 2. The structured search was hindered by the team being directed to search premises which had been identified by calls from members of the public who supplied information to the Police.

The best chance that the Police had to identify those responsible for the robbery was to chase up their regular informants for information. The Metropolitan Police Flying Squad, who were the experts in informant handling, were sent onto the streets to find out what was known. Within twelve hours of the robbery the names (or nicknames) of six of the biggest 'players' in the robbery had been supplied to Detective Superintendent John Cummings, Head of Criminal Intelligence at Scotland Yard.

These names included members of the two gangs that combined to commit the robbery, the South West Gang and the South Coast Raiders, who specialised in stopping trains. It would not have been beyond the wit of the Head of Intelligence at Scotland Yard to extrapolate the other members of the two gangs into a list of suspects. If he had done so, then he would have had the majority of the names that he was seeking.

By the end of August 1963, Commander George Hatherill presented a list of fourteen suspects to the Post Office Investigations Branch. The list included:

Douglas Goody CRO 4290/46
Charles Wilson CRO 5010/54
Bruce Reynolds CRO 41212/48
James White CRO 26113/55

Henry Smith CRO 1551/47
Roy James CRO 17638/56
John Daly CRO 33521/48
Ronald Edwards CRO 33535/61
Thomas Wisbey CRO 26362/47
Danny Pembroke CRO 27206/56
James Hussey CRO 40455/49
Brian Field CRO No Trace
Roger Cordrey CRO 3716/42
Robert Welch CRO 61730/58
Two Post Office men (Irishmen)
From this list Smith and Pembroke were never charged and
Daly was acquitted.

The police received exceptional support from the criminal underworld in their search for the robbers. Some were upset at being ignored by the robbers when they selected their team, so losing out on a share of £2.6 million; others were annoyed at having their criminal activities curtailed by the intense police activity in the weeks following the robbery. It would not have been difficult for them to identify men who were experienced armed robbers and who had disappeared from their usual haunts for over a week and had then been keeping their heads down since then. This covered Objective 1.

The Scenes of Crime officers had already started a sweep of the scene and the collection of the evidence found. It would continue relentlessly provided that the officers received the support and assistance that they required. This covered Objective 3.

A review of the investigation reveals that there were four serious problems with it:

1. Brigadier Cheney, the Chief Constable of Buckinghamshire Police, restricted overtime from the very start of the enquiry – in order to economise on the Police budget – so that manpower was limited throughout the initial enquiries. This meant that when the Forensic Science Team arrived at daybreak on 8 August 1963, the train engine had already been taken back to Crewe by British Rail and local children

had been allowed to climb around in the HVP carriage, obliterating any forensic evidence such as fingerprints.

2. The search for the suspects and their hideout was carried out from the scene to the perimeter, rather than from the perimeter back to the scene. This was an error. The robbers were never going to park up at the end of the road leading from Bridego Bridge. They would want to get as far away as possible in the time available before the crime was reported to the police.

3. The robbers were allowed to stay at Leatherslade Farm for twenty-seven hours after a member of the public contacted Police in Bedfordshire to report that he suspected that the strange men occupying it were the Great Train Robbers. They were also permitted to tidy it up before they left, and it was only due to good fortune that they were not allowed to burn the place down and destroy the evidence that eventually convicted them.

4. The identities of the robbers and their wives and their photos were circulated (on the authority of Commander of the Met CID George Hatherill, upon the recommendation of Detective Chief Superintendent Ernie Millen, the Head of the Met Flying Squad) a few days after the robbery. This led to the robbers, worried about long prison sentences and with pocket-fulls of cash, escaping to all parts of the world, and delayed their apprehension by several years.

The switchboards at Buckinghamshire Police and at New Scotland Yard were both jammed with calls in the days after the robbery, as members of the public attempted to report sightings of the suspects and other important information that they felt that the Police needed to know. Clearly, the police could not respond adequately to all these calls and a screening process needed to be introduced to screen the calls so that the most important calls received the response that they deserved.

The first call from Mr John Marris, a local herdsman, was received at 9.00 am on Monday 12 August 1963, four days after the robbery. He reported that he had seen unusual activity at Leatherslade Farm near Brill on the night of the robbery and suggested that the farm was a likely hideout for the robbers.

Later that same day an estate agent in Bicester in Oxfordshire responded to a request from the police to report all recent property sales to them, calling the Detective Inspector in charge of Oxford City CID to report that he had arranged the sale of Leatherslade Farm a few weeks earlier. The next day two officers were despatched with instructions to visit the farm but returned later to report that they could not find it and that it did not appear on any local maps or on the Ordinance Survey map of the area.

When Commander Hatherill visited Aylesbury Police Station on the morning of 13 August 1963, he asked to see the messages that had been received from the public and noticed Mr Marris' call about Leatherslade Farm. He made enquiries to find out what action had been taken as a result of this message and was told that two officers were on their way there. He reported that he felt some apprehension in case the officers walked into a large gang of robbers at the farm. He did not react proactively. He should have sent reinforcements to the two officers who he appears to have feared were in potentially mortal danger. Instead, he waited rather conservatively for further information to reach him.

Fortunately, the failure of police to respond to his call worried John Marris and he contacted his local station again on Wednesday 14 August 1963 to discuss the matter further. He spoke to a Sergeant Blackman and arranged with him to meet up with the local village bobby, P.C. Wooley, in order to take the officer to the farm to show him what he had seen. In his autobiography, *A Detective's Tale*, George Hatherill records it thus:

'After noon the local policeman at Brill reported by telephone that John Marris had contacted him and that together they had gone to the farm which they had found unoccupied, but in a cellar were some empty mail bags and postal and bank note wrappings.

'Very soon, a cavalcade of police cars was on its way to the farm. It was an ideal hide-out, weedy and desolate, at the end of a narrow lane about a quarter mile from the road, from which the farm, lying below a ridge, was invisible. On one side were three dilapidated sheds, which partly blocked the view of the front; the back and another side were screened by orchards.

'The farm was a two-storey building with five rooms, a large kitchen with a larder, a bathroom, a cellar, where the mail bags and the wrappers had been found. The larder's shelves were stacked like a supermarket, and in the kitchen there was every sort of utensil you could need. An inventory of food in the larder included 18 tins of pork luncheon meet; 9 tins of corned beef; 40 tins of baked beans; 18 one pound packets of butter; 20 tins of peas; 38 tins of soup; 15 tins of condensed milk; 34 tins of fruit salad; 16 two-pound packets of sugar; 7 wrapped loaves of bread; and 19 tins of beer. There were also large supplies of cheese, Oxo, Bovril, ketchup, biscuits, cakes, jam and coffee, half a sack of potatoes, a barrel of apples, a case of oranges, 40 candles, a gas stove, and 17 rolls of toilet paper.

'In the upper rooms there were 11 inflatable rubber mattresses, with blankets and pillows, 6 sleeping bags, 20 jackets, 9 pullovers, several pairs of denim trousers and 20 towels.'

Is it possible that the police made a tactical decision not to invade the farm whilst the robbers were in residence? When the Metropolitan Police was formed in 1829 and for around eighty years after that, officers were armed with heavy lignum vitae wooden truncheons and, when appropriate, cutlasses. When facing armed men, as they did in the armed robbery of a wage delivery in Tottenham in 1911, a case that led to a foot chase across Tottenham and Hackney Marshes and the death of three Constables, officers were permitted to go home and pick up any revolvers, rifles, shotguns and ammunition that they may have there, which in those days did not require a firearms certificate or shotgun certificate.

In the late 1970s, a more professional attitude to firearms was adopted and the Metropolitan Police introduced Ranger 500, the first police vehicle to have posted, permanently-armed, officers available to immediately respond to armed incidents. In the 1980s, this developed into permanently-armed Armed

Response Vehicles (ARVs), which have increased in number and firepower ever since. Of course, control and regulation of these officers and their weapons has also increased.

However in the 1960s, there was an attitude that it was 'bad form' to draw weapons, even when approaching men who were known to possess and use weapons themselves, and officers were encouraged to approach extremely dangerous men without any protection and to talk to them in order to persuade them to surrender their weapons to the officer in the way that the fictional Sergeant George Dixon would have done in *Dixon of Dock Green*.

The prospect of mounting the ridge at Leatherslade Farm to face the fifteen armed robbers who had attacked the train AND their friends and supporters, armed, possibly with the shotguns or handguns that professional armed robbers usually took to work with them and which would have led to a US Waco-type siege with large numbers of robbers and officers dead and injured, would have triggered fear in the heart of most police commanders.

At this time, old time coppers clipped young offenders around the ear and waited around the corner before approaching a disturbance in a pub, until the participants had resolved most of their differences and run out of energy, adrenaline and testosterone, so as to allow the PC to walk in and pick up the tired bodies, and then march them off to the police station. Similarly, ignoring the call from John Marris and letting the robbers leave the farm and make their way back to London, where they could be picked up one-by-one from where they were hiding with their families, might have been considered the wiser option. Certainly, there is no record of any officer being injured whilst arresting any of the suspects for the Great Train Robbery.

Bringing the Robbers to Justice – Their Lives after the Robbery

Roger Cordrey and Bill Boal

The squad made their first arrests just six days after the robbery. Roger Cordrey left Leatherslade Farm on Saturday 10 August

1963 and met up with his old friend, Bill Boal, in Oxford. Cordrey owed Boal a considerable sum of money, and Boal was pressing for it to be returned, but Cordrey told him that he would not repay the money unless Boal accompanied him on a trip to Bournemouth. The two men drove down there with the intention of hiding Cordrey's share of the proceeds of the robbery in two second-hand cars which they proposed to secrete in two lock-up garages.

On Wednesday 14 August 1963 Boal saw an advert for a garage to let in a newsagent's window and the two men went around to visit the person who had placed it, Ethel Clarke, at her home at 45 Tweedale Road in Bournemouth. Mrs Clarke told the two men that she wanted to hire her garage to a local person rather than to a visitor to the town, but they pressed her to reconsider. Unfortunately for them, Mrs Clarke, 67, was the widow of a former local police officer and she became suspicious at their determination to hire the garage and their willingness to pay an exorbitant rent for it, in advance, in cash, in used ten-shilling notes, and she cunningly sent the two men away to collect their vehicle with instructions for them return to the house in one hour in order to collect the spare key to the garage.

By the time that the two men returned at 9.00 pm, two of Mrs Clark's husband's former colleagues, Detective Sergeant Stanley Davies and Detective Constable Charles Case, were waiting for them. Keys found in Boal's possession opened an Austin A35 saloon motor car index number UEL987 parked in the garage at Tweedale Road and a search of the vehicle revealed a bag containing used banknotes totalling £56,047. The two men were arrested and taken to Bournemouth Police Station.

It was at the Police Station where, a little after midnight, Boal was found to be in possession of another car key to a vehicle index number TLX 279, which was parked in a garage at 59 Eastbury Avenue in Bournemouth. When this was searched, more used banknotes to the value of £78,982 were found. A few minutes later Cordrey collapsed in agony and admitted to the police that he had hidden the other key to this vehicle up his rectum and a forensic medical examiner, Dr M.J. Saunders of 61 Grove Road in Bournemouth, had to be summoned to the police station to remove it.

Finally, at 3 am, Police searched a flat at 935 Wimborne Road in Bournemouth where, in a bedroom, they found a briefcase containing £840 and a total of £5,910, making a total of £141,017. Both Cordrey and Boal admitted that the money was the proceeds of the Great Train Robbery and the total sum recovered in Bournemouth would have been only a little less than the sum of £150,000 that the squad had calculated to be the size of a share of the proceeds, if there had been seventeen equal shares and a variety of 'drinks' paid from it.

Cordrey was already a suspect for the robbery and officers from the squad were despatched to Bournemouth to bring the two men, together with the money found in their possession, back to London, where they were interviewed by Detective Superintendent Malcolm Fewtrell and Detective Sergeant Jack Pritchard. Other officers were despatched to search both men's London addresses and Boal's wife Rene, and his sister May Florence Pilgrim, and her husband Alfred Pilgrim, were arrested for Receiving Stolen Money.

Being found with an amount of money that it would have taken him a century to earn in his regular job provided good evidence to support a charge against Cordrey and the interview would have proved his links to the other robbers and to the robbery plot. He was charged with Conspiracy to Rob and Receiving Stolen Property and at his trial at Aylesbury Crown Court in April 1964 he was sentenced to a total of 20 years imprisonment, which was reduced to 14 years on appeal.

He was released in 1971. He moved to the West Country where he returned to the flower business and lived a quiet life. Throughout his life Cordrey was neurotic, with other deeper emotional problems, and these did not improve as he got older.

Boal was charged with Receiving Stolen Goods and gaoled for 24 years, which was reduced to 14 years on appeal. Frank Williams expressed the view that Boal was a member of the South Coast Raiders Gang and that he was the man responsible for identifying ways of uncoupling train carriages following a robbery. Since his arrest, several Robbers have denied having ever met Boal and it is now widely accepted that Boal played no part in the actual robbery. Perhaps the most telling evidence of this is the fact that although the two men were arrested together within six days of the Robbery, only one share of the proceeds was found in their possession. Boal died of cancer in gaol in 1970.

Charlie Wilson

Charlie Wilson was the first member of the gang to be targeted by the squad. His name had been 'propped-up' by informants within forty-eight hours of the robbery. He was known to be an active armed robber and was known to associate with other suspects for the robbery. Whilst most of the others had 'had it on their toes' and run away, Wilson had stayed at home and continued with his normal life and so was easy to find and arrest.

On 22 August 1963, two weeks after the robbery, at 12.55 pm, Detective Sergeant Nigel Reid from the Flying Squad was waiting at Wilson's home address at 45 Crescent Lane, Clapham, London SW4, when he came home. He detained Wilson at the address until Detective Inspector Byers and Detective Sergeant John Vaughan arrived at the address at 1.20 pm and arrested Wilson. DS Reid then stayed with Wilson whilst DI Byers and DS Vaughan searched the address. It is interesting to note that the officers were not in possession of a search warrant and that they did not caution Wilson, either whilst at his home, or in the police car on their way to Cannon Row Police Station, adjoining New Scotland Yard. The law at that time required Police officers to secure a search warrant from a magistrate before entering or searching premises, but the majority of searches during the enquiry were conducted without a warrant. Butler was paranoid about security and may have felt that with the support of the Home Secretary and Prime Minister he did not require one in order to secure convictions.

Upon his arrival at the police station, Wilson was interviewed by Detective Chief Superintendent Tommy Butler and Detective Chief Inspector Baldock and denied ever have been to the Cheddington area or knowing anything about the robbery. When told by Butler that he was being taken to Aylesbury to be charged and then cautioned, Wilson is alleged to have said that he did not know how they hoped to make the charges stick 'without the poppy' (money), a statement picked up by the press and which became the subject of considerable debate in the press.

Wilson's fingerprints had been found on the windowsill in the kitchen of Leatherslade Farm, on a drum of salt and on a Johnson's First Aid Travel Kit found at the farm. He was charged with Armed Robbery and Conspiracy to Rob and at his trial at Aylesbury Crown Court in April 1964 he, together with nine of the other fifteen members of the robbery gang, was sentenced to a total of 30 years imprisonment. His refusal to speak throughout the trial led to his being labelled as 'The Silent Man'.

Following his conviction, Wilson was held at HMP Winson Green where, after just four months, on 12 August 1964, he arranged for a three-man gang to break into the prison to break him out. Wilson and his family then settled in Rigaud, situated between Montreal and Ottawa, in Canada. He later moved between Mexico, Canada and the South of France, but having successfully evaded capture for four years, Wilson was eventually caught on 24 January 1968, when his wife telephoned her parents in England and enabled Scotland Yard to trace the call and track them down.

Following his return to England, Wilson served ten more years in the train robbers' secure unit at HMP Durham, before he became the final train robber to emerge from prison for the robbery in 1978. Following his return, Wilson moved to Marbella, Spain and returned to a life of crime, quickly becoming a suspect in a £100 million gold fraud, although he was never charged in connection with it. He was later suspected of involvement in Armed Robbery, Drug Smuggling, Money Laundering and Fraud.

He was engaged to launder some of the proceeds from the Brink's-MAT robbery, which occurred early on 26 November 1983, when six robbers broke into the Brink's-MAT warehouse at Heathrow Airport, London, and stole £26 million. Wilson lost the Brink's-MAT robbers £3 million, so that on 23 April 1990 a young South London man knocked on the front door of his hacienda, north of Marbella, and shot Wilson and his pet German Shepherd dog at point-blank range, before riding off down the hill on a yellow bicycle. Over the next three years, four more shootings were connected to the Brink's-MAT raid.

Gordon Goody

Gordon Goody was arrested and charged with the robbery at the BOAC offices at Comet House near Heathrow Airport in 1962. The case against him was largely based on forensic evidence found at the scene and he was eventually acquitted. As the jury filed out of the court, Goody walked over to the table where the evidence was sitting and picked up a chain that had been used to secure a gate blocking a road leading away from Comet House, which had been used by the robbers. He picked up the chain and showed the forensic experts what they had missed, that the robbers had inserted a dummy link in the chain so that it could be easily broken to allow the robbers to use the road to make good their escape. He therefore humiliated the forensic scientists so that, when he became a suspect for the Great Train Robbery, the scientists were highly motivated to provide the evidence necessary to convict him and restore their reputations.

Although Goody's was the first name on the list of suspects that Tommy Butler had delivered to the Post Office Investigations Branch on 16 August 1963, his fingerprints were not found at Leatherslade Farm and accordingly his name did not appear on the list of suspects supplied to the media on 22 August 1963. In the intervening week the squad had searched his mother's home and this clearly worried him so that he moved into the Windmill Public House at 17 Upper Ground in Blackfriars in Central London and wrote to the officer in the BOAC case in the following terms:

22/8/63

Dear Sir,

No doubt you will be surprised to hear from me after my double trial at the Old Bailey for the London Airport Robbery.

At the time of writing I am not living at my home address because it seems that I am a suspect in the recent train robbery. Two Flying Squad officers recently visited my home address whilst I was out, and made a search of the premises and honestly Mr Osborne, I am now very worried that they connect me with this crime. The reason I write to you now is because you always treated me in a straight forward manner during the Airport Case. I will never forget how fair and just yourself and Mr Field were towards me.

That case took nearly eight months to finish and every penny I had, and to become a suspect in the last big robbery is more than I can stand.

So my intentions are to keep out of harm's way until the people concerned in the train robbery are found.

To some people this letter would seem like a sign of guilt, but all I am interested in is keeping my freedom.

Hoping these few lines find you and Mr Field in the best of health.

Yours faithfully,
D.G. Goody

On hearing of Wilson's arrest, Goody panicked and decided to borrow both the landlord's name and his car, rather than using his own cars (a Jaguar and a Ford Zodiac) which were known to the police. He headed north up the M1 to the Grand Hotel in Leicester, to visit his girlfriend, Margaret Perkins. He broke down in Cranfield, near Bedford and was compelled to hire a car to complete the journey.

On Friday 23 August 1963, the day after Wilson's arrest and just two weeks after the robbery, Goody was mistaken for Bruce Reynolds, whose picture had just appeared in the national press. Police were called and he was arrested at the hotel and taken to Leicester City Police Headquarters where at 3.15 pm he was interviewed by Detective Chief Inspector Peter Vibart and Detective Sergeant Read of the Flying Squad. He denied ever being in Cheddington or being involved in the robbery, claiming that he was in Ireland at the time of the robbery. He was taken to Aylesbury Police Station where he arrived shortly before midnight and was interviewed three times by Tommy Butler in the next twenty-four hours, before being released on bail to return on 7 September.

Whilst Goody was detained at Leicester City Police Headquarters, Detective Sergeant John Vaughan of the Flying Squad, the same officer who had searched Wilson's address the previous day, searched Goody's room on the second floor of the

Windmill Public House, where he was known to be friends of the management and to have recently stayed, as he had done for many years. He was known to have his own room above the public house and to keep a change of clothing there. Among the articles found in his room were a pair of brown suede Truform size ten shoes, with criss-crossed, rubber, patterned soles, and following this the officers then decided to move on to search the rest of the premises.

Convinced by Goody's guilt and frustrated by their inability to charge him, the squad decided to review his case. They decided to compare yellow paint found on the shoes found at The Windmill with paint seen at Leatherslade Farm and on 28 August 1963 Detective Constable Keith Milner was sent to the farm to collect the tin of yellow paint that he had seen there on 14 August 1963 but the significance of which he had failed to recognise. He then gave both the paint splattered shoes and the tin of paint to Dr Ian Holden for comparison.

On 7 September 1963, Dr Holden had not yet completed his forensic tests and Goody's bail was extended for four weeks until 3 October 1963, at Putney Police Station, where he was briefly interviewed by the 'Terrible Twins', Detective Chief Superintendent Tommy Butler and Detective Chief Inspector Peter Vibart, and re-bailed to 10 October 1963 at Aylesbury Police Station, where he was charged with Armed Robbery and Conspiracy to Rob.

Goody stood trial at Aylesbury Crown Court in April 1964, together with nine of the other fifteen members of the robbery gang. At the trial Dr Ian Holden of the Metropolitan Police Laboratory at New Scotland Yard, testified that on 26 August 1963 he examined the shoes and found that they bore traces of yellow and khaki paint. He then compared this paint with samples of paint taken from a tin of yellow paint which had been found at the farm, and found it to be similar but not identical. Next Holden compared the khaki paint from the shoes with the khaki paint from the Land Rover and found that these were identical. When Holden compared the paint from the yellow lorry to the paint in the tin he found that it was similar. When Holden examined the two Land Rovers he discovered minute traces of both khaki and yellow paint on the pedals.

Holden found that both paints were identical to those found on the shoes, although it was impossible for him to confirm that the same shoes had put the paint onto the pedals. Finally, Dr Holden found traces of yellow paint that had been spilt at the farm, mixed into the gravel and with mineral content. When analysed, a sample of this was found to be identical to the paint found on the shoes and on the pedals. Together, these results had successfully established a link between the shoes, the wearer of the shoes and Leatherslade Farm.

Goody called the managers of the Windmill Public House, Mr and Mrs Alexander, to give evidence at his trial. They testified that the shoes had been pristinely clean when the Police removed them from the hotel following the search. He also called his own, equally eminent scientist to contradict many of Dr Holden's findings, and felt that he had negated Holden's evidence, which was the basis of the Prosecution case. But as he was convicted, it is clear that Holden's testimony prevailed.

Goody was sentenced to a total of 30 years imprisonment and following his release in 1975 he moved to Spain and opened a bar. He has remained there ever since.

Recently, Gordon Goody claimed that he had been framed by the police, and told the *Daily Mirror*, "They weren't the shoes I'd worn for the train. I wore desert boots. They took my brown suede shoes from my mum's and they appeared at court, complete with yellow paint. The judge knew I'd been fitted up." A sympathetic reader would realise that Goody was making these allegations more than fifty years after the robbery, and that at 85 years of age, his memory was failing. Others would claim that this was a complete and utter fabrication, and bore no relation to the truth.

Ronnie Biggs

Ronnie Biggs was tasked with looking after 'Pops' during and after the robbery. The retired train driver, whom Biggs had introduced to the gang, was supposed to move the engine on after the HVP carriage had been uncoupled from the rest of the train, but was a little absent-minded and needed to be chivvied along.

Biggs received a visit from the police on Saturday 24 August 1963 at 6.45pm. He had told his wife Charmian that he had been offered a job cutting down trees in Wiltshire. While he was away, a relative died and Charmian tried to contact Biggs, but was unable to do so as he was away committing the Great Train Robbery. She called the police to seek their help in tracing Biggs to inform him of the death. (She was innocent of the ways of the underworld. If Reynolds', Goody's or Wilson's wives had felt the need to trace their husbands, they would have done nothing but wait, as they knew the rules of the game of armed robbery).

The Metropolitan Police Flying Squad knew Biggs as a small time thief, but they were interested to hear that he had been away from home at the time of the Robbery and that he had lied to his wife about where he was going. The Flying Squad did not feel that Biggs was of sufficient status to be a serious suspect for the Robbery, but took the precaution of asking Surrey Police to 'have a word' with him, just to be on the safe side. Detective Inspector Basil Morris and Detective Sergeant Church, both attached to Surrey Police, visited him at the request of the Flying Squad and briefly questioned him about his knowledge of the robbery. During the interview Biggs admitted to Morris that he knew Bruce Reynolds "from inside".

Following the failure to burn down Leatherslade Farm, and the discovery of his fingerprints on a Heinz Tomato Ketchup bottle, on a Pyrex plate and on a Monopoly box lid, all found at the farm after the robbers had left, a warrant was issued for his arrest. On 4 September 1963 at 2.45 pm Detective Inspector Frank Williams arrived with a squad of officers at Biggs' home address at 37, Alpine Road, Redhill in Surrey. Biggs was not there but his wife, Charmian was just about to take their children to the doctor's. Williams sent three of his officers to accompany them and when they returned a full forensic search of the premises was underway. At 6.20 pm Biggs returned to the address and was arrested and conveyed to New Scotland Yard.

Following an interview by Detective Chief Superintendent Tommy Butler, Biggs was taken to Aylesbury Police Station, where he was charged with Armed Robbery and Conspiracy to Rob and at his trial at Aylesbury Crown Court in April 1964 he, together with nine of the other fifteen members of the robbery gang, was sentenced to a total of 30 years imprisonment.

Biggs served fifteen months before escaping from HMP Wandsworth on 8 July 1965, scaling the wall with a rope ladder and dropping onto a waiting removal van. He fled to Brussels by boat, then sent a note to his wife telling her to join him in Paris, where he had acquired new identity papers and was undergoing plastic surgery. During his time in prison, Charmian had started an extra-marital relationship so that she was pregnant by the time he escaped to the Continent. Choosing to support her husband, she had an abortion in London and then travelled with their two sons to Paris to join him.

In 1966 Biggs fled to Sydney, Australia, but by the time his family followed him there later that year, all but £7,000 of his share of the proceeds from the robbery had been spent, £40,000 on plastic surgery in Paris, £55,000 paid to get him out of the UK and into Australia; the rest on legal fees and expenses. The next year Biggs received an anonymous letter from Britain telling him that Interpol suspected that he was in Australia and that he should move on.

Three weeks later, he landed in Panama and within two weeks he had flown to Brazil, which did not have an extradition treaty with the UK. In 1974 *Daily Express* reporter Colin MacKenzie received information suggesting that Biggs was in Rio de Janeiro. Detective Chief Superintendent Jack Slipper of the Flying Squad, a member of the original investigating team for the robbery arrived soon afterwards, accompanied by Detective Sergeant Peter Jones, also of the Flying Squad.

Slipper found that Biggs could not be extradited because his girlfriend, nightclub dancer Raimunda de Castro, was pregnant. Brazilian law at that time did not allow a parent of a Brazilian child to be extradited. In 1997 the UK and Brazil ratified an extradition treaty and two months later, the UK Government made a formal request to the Brazilians for Biggs's extradition and Biggs stated that he would no longer oppose extradition. However, the Brazilian Supreme Court rejected the extradition request and gave Biggs the right to live in Brazil for the rest of his life.

In 2001 Biggs announced to *The Sun* newspaper that he would be willing to return to the UK. Biggs arrived on 7 May 2001, whereupon he was immediately arrested and re-imprisoned. In a press release his son, Michael, said that Biggs did not return to the UK simply to receive health care which was unavailable in Brazil, but that it was his desire to 'walk into a Margate pub as an Englishman and buy a pint of bitter'.

After a series of health problems, appeals for early release and prison transfers, Biggs was finally released from custody on 6 August 2009, two days before his 80th birthday, on compassionate grounds. On 18 December 2013, aged 84, Biggs died at the Carlton Court Care Home in Barnet, north London.

Tommy Wisbey

Tommy Wisbey was originally interviewed shortly after the robbery, when the squad realised that he and his wife Rene were close friends with Buster and June Edwards and since that time his home at 27 Ayton House, Elmington Estate, Camberwell SE5 had been kept under constant observation. When his left palm print was found on a chrome handrail in the bathroom at Leatherslade Farm, police had not seen him for about a week, but decided to wait for him to surface rather than include his name and photograph in the press release with the other suspects.

Frank Williams decided that Wisbey may be hiding inside his home and decided to search it on 7 September 1963 at 7 am. The front door was answered by Rene Wisbey, who made tea whilst the officers searched the place, and then tearfully explained to them that Tommy had taken up with another woman and taken her to Spain on holiday. Williams, not taken in for one moment by Rene's performance, but with no other options, thanked her for the tea and returned to his office at New Scotland Yard. Four days later, he received a call there from Wisbey, who clearly believed that Williams lacked any evidence to justify his arrest and simply wanted another chat about Edwards. They agreed to meet at Wisbey's betting shop in half an hour.

So it was that on 11 September 1963 at 11.30am Detective Inspector Frank Williams and Detective Sergeant Stanley Moore of the Flying Squad met Tommy Wisbey at his betting shop in Red Cross Road, London SE1. They then took him to New Scotland Yard where Steve Moore took his palmprints. This was necessary as Wisbey had been wearing gloves at the farm, but due to the heavy manual work of carrying the mail sacks, etc., the gloves had shrunk and ridden up his hands, revealing the butts of his hand, which were the prints that had been found at the farm. By re-taking Wisbey's prints, Steve Moore could 'prove' the prints without reference to another officer who may not be easily available, and could focus on the area around the butt of his hand, so as to improve the quality of the evidence available to the court.

Wisbey was questioned by Tommy Butler and denied ever having been to Cheddington or of being involved in the robbery. He claimed to be in the Newington Arms Public House in King and Queen Street, Walworth, London SE17, talking to the licensee, William Edward Coupland on the evening before the robbery and to be at home with his father and brothers on the night of the robbery. Unfortunately for him, none of these people supported his alibi when questioned by police. Accordingly, he was taken to Aylesbury Police Station where he was charged with Armed Robbery and Conspiracy to Rob and at his trial at Aylesbury Crown Court in April 1964 he, together with nine of the other fifteen members of the robbery gang, was sentenced to a total of 30 years imprisonment.

Wisbey was eventually released in 1976, and after a period spent working as a car dealer, he returned to a life of crime and in 1989 was convicted of Supplying Cocaine and sentenced to a term of ten years imprisonment.

Jim Hussey

Jim Hussey assumed the position of 'heavy' at the robbery. After the crime he was one of the early suspects for the robbery and his home was kept under surveillance for four weeks. Despite Hussey not showing any signs of spending money or behaving suspiciously, on 7 September 1963 a decision was made to search his address and take him in for questioning. Accordingly, Detective Sergeants Jim Nevill and Jack Slipper were sent to Hussey's address at 8 Edridge House, Dog Kennel Hill in East Dulwich, London SE22.

At 11 am Hussey was interviewed by Tommy Butler and after denying knowing anything about the robbery, Leatherslade Farm or any of the robbers, he was asked to supply his palm prints and readily agreed to do so. The prints were taken and delivered to Detective Superintendent Maurice Ray, who was in charge of the Forensic Science team at Leatherslade Farm. He had a number of unidentified prints and over the next hour or so he checked these against the prints supplied by Hussey.

At 1 pm Hussey was again seen by Butler who asked him if he had seen any Land Rovers or Austin vans recently and when Hussey told him that he had not, Butler told him that he would be conveyed to Aylesbury Police Station to be charged with Armed Robbery and Conspiracy to Rob. His right palm print had been found on the tailboard of the Austin lorry used in the robbery. At his trial at Aylesbury Crown Court in April 1964 he, together with nine of the other fifteen members of the robbery gang, was sentenced to a total of 30 years imprisonment.

Following his release from prison, Hussey promptly married his girlfriend, Gill, before working on a flower stall and then opening up a restaurant in Soho in Central London. However, crime followed him and he was soon convicted of assault in 1981 and then gaoled for seven years in 1989, when he was found guilty with fellow gang member, Tommy Wisbey, of dealing cocaine.

Jim Hussey passed away in St. Christopher's Hospice in Sydenham in South London on 12 November 2012. It was here, on his deathbed, that he confessed to being the robber who coshed train driver Jack Mills during the robbery. However this is regarded with scepticism by many people, who believe that he was merely admitting to it in order to protect another gang member.

Lennie Field

Lennie Field was a merchant seaman and met Brian Field (no relation) when Brian assisted the solicitor who represented Lennie's brother, Alexander, at court. Alexander was convicted and sentenced to a term of imprisonment so Brian assisted Alexander to secure a power of attorney for Lennie to manage his (Alexander's) affairs, while Alexander was in prison.

Brian recognised Lennie to be the ideal person to act on behalf of the robbers in the purchase of Leatherslade Farm. Brian accompanied Lennie when he went to view the farm and meet the seller. They made an offer of £5,550 for the purchase of the farm, and Lennie persuaded the owner to allow him access to the farm upon the payment of a 10% deposit so that he could undertake improvements to the property before he completed the purchase by paying the remainder of the sum agreed, and moved into the farm. Of course, once the robbery had taken place and the farm had been used as a getaway and the robbers had no further use of it, the sale never went through and the owner never received the money.

Witnesses saw people working at the farm on 6 and 7 August, the days before the robbery; it was probably the gang members delivering their supplies and making their final preparations.

Several weeks later, Police interviewed Brian Field at his brother's home address. He provided a cover story that implicated Lennie Field as the purchaser of the farm and his boss, John Wheater, as the conveyancer. He admitted visiting the farm with Lennie Field, but said that he assumed that it was intended as an investment for Lennie's brother, Alexander Field.

Lennie Field was arrested on 14 September 1963 at his home address, and charged with Conspiracy to Rob and Obstructing Justice. Later, at the Crown Court, he was convicted and sentenced to a total of 25 years imprisonment. Following his release from prison, Lennie disappeared from public view.

Brian Field

On Friday 16 August 1963, just eight days after the robbery, at 8.35 am John Aherne was riding his motorcycle through Dorking Woods in Surrey, with Mrs Esa Nina Hargreaves as a pillion passenger. The motorbike engine started to cut out and Aherne decided to park it up and wait for it to cool down. The couple decided to go for a walk while they waited, but after a very short distance they discovered a briefcase, a holdall and a camel-skin bag, all containing money. They called police, who discovered another briefcase, full of money, nearby. In total, a sum of £100,900 was found. Inside another camel-skin bag they found a receipt from the Café Restaurant in Pension Sonnenbichl, Allgau, Austria. It was made out in favour of a Herr and Frau Field. Surrey Police delivered it all to Fewtrell and McArthur in Aylesbury.

By this time the Flying Squad team at Scotland Yard investigating the robbery had heard about Brian Field. They knew that he was a clerk at James and Wheater (Solicitors), the company which had acted for the purchaser of Leatherslade Farm. They quickly confirmed, through Interpol, that Brian and Karin Field had stayed at the Pension Sonnenbichl in February of that year.

Several weeks later, Police interviewed Field at his home address. He provided a cover story that implicated Lennie Field as the purchaser of the farm and his boss, John Wheater, as the conveyancer. He admitted visiting the farm with Lennie Field, but said that he assumed that it was intended as an investment for Lennie's brother, Alexander Field.

Brian Field, not knowing that Police had found the receipt, readily confirmed that he and his wife had been to Germany on a holiday and provided the details of the hotel where they stayed, which was the hotel named on the receipt. Brian Field was arrested at his home address on 15 September 1963.

Brian Field was charged with Conspiracy to Rob and Obstructing Justice and at his trial at Aylesbury Crown Court in April 1964 he appeared with nine of the other fifteen members of the robbery gang, and was sentenced to a total of 25 years imprisonment. At the trial it was also alleged that he was the crucial link between the 'Ulsterman' who came up with the idea of robbing the train, and that he provided the robbers with much of the information that they needed in order to commit the robbery. Field was originally convicted on both charges that he faced, but the conviction for Conspiracy to Rob was later overturned on appeal, leaving him convicted of Obstructing Justice and facing a term of five years imprisonment.

Field served his sentence and was released in 1967. Whilst in prison, his wife divorced him and upon his release he got remarried, to a younger woman, Sian. On 27 April 1979 Field and his new wife were both killed in a road traffic accident on the M4 motorway.

The 'Ulsterman' – Patrick McKenna?

Since the robbery in 1963, the world has been speculating on the identity of the Ulsterman who supplied the inside information that led to the Great Train Robbery. On 29 September 2014, Gordon Goody, the robber who was allegedly approached by the Ulsterman and thereafter managed him, identified him as a 43-year-old man from Belfast called 'Paddy'!!! (and then supplied the surname McKenna, another very popular Irish name). He went on to say that McKenna was a Catholic and that, as far as anybody who knows him is aware, he never spent any of his £150,000 share of the proceeds of the robbery and that the best guess is that he probably gave it all the church. As any donation of £5,000 would be specifically recorded and questions asked about its origin, this is highly unlikely and it is more likely that he buried it and never went back for it because he was frightened of getting caught.

John Wheater

John Wheater was a former soldier and Brian Field's employer at the firm of James and Wheater (Solicitors), the company which acted for Lennie Field in the purchase of Leatherslade Farm. Wheater was a weak and feeble man who was dominated and controlled by Brian Field. Despite Wheater being a qualified solicitor and owning his own company, Brian Field earned considerably more, and had a far bigger house and car than Wheater.

Although the squad officers personally believed that it would have been impossible for Wheater to not know what Brian Field had been doing – selling addresses of rich clients with property worth stealing to those who had been charged with stealing, and setting up robberies and burglaries and taking a fee for doing so – Wheater denied this and the squad was unable to prove otherwise.

John Wheater was arrested at his home address on 17 September 1963, and charged with Obstructing Justice. He was the last of the nine defendants to enter the dock at Aylesbury Crown Court in April 1964. Judge Edmund Davies described Wheater's case as 'the saddest and most difficult of all', and Wheater as 'the man whose conviction had been a personal and professional disaster'. For Wheater, guilty only of conspiring to conceal the identity of the buyer of Leatherside Farm, the raiders' hideout, the sentence was three years imprisonment. He disappeared from public view following his release from prison.

Roy James

Roy James' role in the robbery was to uncouple the HVP carriage from the rest of the train, and after the robbery to drive one of the Land Rovers from the scene of the robbery at Cheddington to the hideout at Leatherslade Farm in Brill.

On 7 December 1963, four months after the robbery, a female informant called the squad office at New Scotland Yard to report that Roy James was hiding out at 14 Ryder's Terrace, St John's Wood in North London, near the Abbey Road Studios where in September 1969 the Beatles would record their album of the same name. She spoke to Tommy Butler and was able to tell him the steps that James had taken to alter his appearance, by losing weight and growing a beard, the escape route over the roofs of the flats that James had established in case police visited the flat, and the details of the Jaguar E Type saloon that had parked nearby to assist his escape.

She then went on to demand that her personal details remained confidential so as to protect her from the potentially violent consequences her disclosure might provoke from James or his friends. She did, however, specifically state that the same particulars could be forwarded to the Post Office Investigations Branch if it assisted her claim for the reward due for James' capture.

Detective Sergeants Jack Slipper and Jim Nevill were then tasked with arranging for the area around the flats to be scouted so that potential difficulties were identified and resolved before any attempt was made to capture James. They approached St Marylebone borough engineer for details of drains and sewers etc., and despatched female officers to peruse the area as it was felt that in those days they would attract less suspicion than male officers.

An area twenty feet square was identified as having been ploughed to a depth of several feet in order to provide a soft landing area adjacent to Blenheim Terrace, which it was suspected that James, an accomplished cat burglar, had prepared in order to assist in his escape. Tommy Butler posted five officers to surround this area when the other officers entered the flat to arrest James.

When satisfied that he had taken all necessary precautions and made all possible preparations, Detective Chief Superintendent

Tommy Butler led his own team of 'cat burglars' up to the flat to arrest James. It was a specially selected squad of athletic officers including Detective Sergeants Nevill, Moore, Matthews and Price as well as PC 99 D Lewis and PC 586 D O'Loughlin from the local St John's Wood Police Station. WPC Willey, who was working with the Flying Squad on the robbery enquiry, attempted to draw James to the front door by deceit, but when this failed Tommy Butler resorted to loud banging and then gave instructions for the rest of the team to force entry to the flat.

DS Neville and DS Moore climbed onto the balcony and smashed a window that gave them access to one of the bedrooms, where they saw James disappear through a fanlight onto the roof of the premises, carrying a holdall. The officers followed James across the roofs and saw him jump onto the pre-prepared soft landing area, where he was grabbed by DS Moore and the two PCs.

When arrested and cautioned by the officers, James accurately summed up his situation when he replied, 'Well that's it. I suppose I am lucky to be alive,' (presumably after the chase over the roofs?). He immediately disowned the bag and its contents, £12.041 in used banknotes together with a note which appeared to be an account of £109,500, which the officers believed was an account of his share of the proceeds of the robbery. When searched, James was found to have another £131 10s in his wallet.

The evidence against James related to the finding of his fingerprints on a blue Pyrex plate, a Johnson's First Aid Travel Kit, and on a loose page of an American magazine, Movie Screen, all left behind at Leatherslade Farm when the robbers fled. James was charged with Armed Robbery and Conspiracy to Rob and at his trial at Aylesbury Crown Court in April 1964 he, together with nine of the other fifteen members of the robbery gang, was sentenced to a total of 30 years imprisonment.

He served just eleven years before being released in 1975. James went straight back to motor racing, but his hopes of being a Formula 1 driver were dashed after a series of crashes, so he returned to his former trade as a silversmith, producing trophies for the Formula 1 World Championship. Roy James was a friend of Bernie Ecclestone, which, incidentally, led to rumours that

Ecclestone himself was an investor in the Robbery, but he has denied them.

In 1983, James was accused of attempting to import gold without paying excise duty on it, along with fellow gang member, Charlie Wilson. Although acquitted of this offence, James did not stay out of trouble for long and was sentenced to six years imprisonment after shooting his father-in-law and hitting his wife with the pistol. After three years in prison he underwent triple-bypass surgery and was released in 1997, only to die soon after from another heart attack, aged just 62.

Bob Welch

Bob Welch was employed as a heavy intended to intimidate the staff on the train into complying with the demands made by the robbers during the robbery. Immediately after the robbery he remained at home and kept to his usual routine, but as the pressure mounted on the robbers he went missing. It was later discovered that he had moved to Cornwall, where he had been staying at the Harbour Lights Hotel in Mevagissey from 30 August 1963 to 8 September 1963 before he moved to the Headland Hotel in Newquay until 13 September.

Mr R.F. Yates of the Post Office Investigation Branch (POIB) then traced Welch and others to an isolated farm near Beaford in Devon, where he was told there was also £200,000 from the proceeds of the robbery. Mr Yates confided his suspicions to the local Postmaster and his wife as well as to the local postman. He then sought their help in identifying the details of those at the farm, their vehicles, finance and habits and in supporting the POIB team that he had despatched to the area. The men at the farm were identified as:

Charles Lilley CRO 27967/42
John Sturm CRO 19274/54
Ronald Harvey CRO 1196/51
Bobby Welch CRO 61730/58
Danny Pembroke CRO 27206/56

A check of the telephone showed a sudden and unexpected rise in the frequency and duration of calls made from the number and indicated that the new occupants had moved into the premises on 17 September 1963, shortly after Welch left the hotel in Newquay.

A tap on the telephone revealed that a substantial number of calls were being made from the number, mainly to the occupants' home addresses in London or to betting shops in the London area. Three calls attracted particular attention. The day after their arrival, on 18 September 1963, at 9 am a call lasting 3 minutes and 9 seconds was made to Lincoln and Lincoln (Solicitors) in Armitage Road in London NW1. At 4.38 pm on the same day a call lasting two minutes and one second was made to Whitehall 1212, the number of New Scotland Yard. A little over an hour later at 5.58 pm another call, lasting six minutes and two seconds, was made to the same number. So who was calling New Scotland Yard and why?

The POIB surveillance team watched the address and the suspects for a couple of weeks, as they went hunting, shooting and fishing and 'flashed the cash' on drinking, gambling and shopping. Eventually, Williams became satisfied that no further suspects were likely to join the group and that no further useful information would be obtained by continuing the observation and requested approval to raid the premises, arrest Welch and search for evidence. He was overruled by Tommy Butler and the surveillance continued.

Eventually the squad received information from an informant that Welch was to travel up to London and on Friday 25 October 1963 a team of five officers were despatched to London Bridge Station, where at 8.50 pm Detective Inspector Frank Williams and Detective Sergeant Lou van Dyck stopped Welch. He was arrested and taken to Cannon Row Police Station, where he was interviewed by Tommy Butler and named Charles Lilley and Jimmy Kensit as his alibi witnesses. But whilst Lilley made a statement supporting this alibi, Kensit denied all knowledge of meeting Welch on the day of the robbery.

At 3.00 pm the next day he was told that he was being taken to Aylesbury Police Station to be charged with Armed Robbery and Conspiracy to Rob. At his trial Welch faced evidence that his left and right palm prints had both been found on a can of Pipkin ale found at Leatherslade Farm. In April 1964 he appeared at Aylesbury Crown Court, together with nine of the other fifteen members of the robbery gang, and was sentenced to a total of 30 years imprisonment.

Following his release from prison on 14 June 1976, he moved back in with his wife, June, and his son, and retrieved the remainder of his money from the man who had been left in charge of it, by the use of threats. Following his release he became a car dealer and gambler in London. He was once suspected of dishonestly handling diamonds but was cleared of the charge.

In later life he was left crippled following a botched operation on his leg, intended to help an injury that he had sustained whilst in prison, so he had to attend Bruce Reynolds' funeral in a wheelchair.

John Daly

John Daly was the brother-in-law of Bruce Reynolds, who considered him to be his lucky talisman. In the robbery he was employed in assisting Roger Cordrey with the dwarf signal while Cordrey dealt with the main signal.

Daly was identified as a suspect for the Great Train Robbery within twelve hours of the robbery taking place, and the fact that he was related to Bruce Reynolds would not have helped him to allay that suspicion. The squad received reliable information that Daly had divided his share of the proceeds of the robbery into three equal parts and given these to three of his friends, William Goodwin, Michael Black and a jeweller from Folkestone, for them to look after. He soon learned that criminals cannot be trusted, even by their so-called friends.

The day after the robbery Daly visited several boatyards on the Isle of Wight and enquired about buying a 9 ton boat. He stated that he had £25,000 to spend on it and gave his name as Mr Grant of 83 Sloane Square in London. DI Frank Williams then heard that Daly had taken the family to Margate, but fearing that door-to-door enquiries would spook them and cause them to run, he instigated discreet enquiries that placed the family at the Endcliffe Hotel in First Avenue in Cliftonville. But on 26 August 1963 John Daly asked for his bill and checked out of the hotel, citing his wife's problems with her pregnancy. Williams later discovered that the publication of his name and photo in the media had caused the family to run before he could get officers down there to arrest Daly.

Daly returned to London and sent his child away to friends. He and his wife went into hiding in the basement of a house at 65A Eaton Square. He grew a beard and went on a severe fish-only diet that dramatically changed his appearance. An informant supplied this address to the squad and arrangements were made for it to be raided.

On 3 December 1963 at 4.15 pm Tommy Butler led a team consisting of Frank Williams, Detective Sergeant Steve Moore, Detective Sergeant Bernard Price and Detective Constable John Estenson down the steps to the flat and gave the secret ring of two short rings followed by a long ring and the front door was answered by Mrs Daly. The officers stormed into the flat and Daly jumped to his feet and identified himself as Paul Grant. But when Frank Willams said, 'Now come on, you remember me', he replied, 'Hello Mr Williams. I'm caught.'

Daly was then taken to Scotland Yard by Butler, Williams, Moore and Price, while the other officers were left to search the flat and interview anybody who might have been assisting Daly to remain at large. The officers seized a quantity of correspondence belonging to a man called Michael Black, including his driving licence, firearm certificate, items of personal correspondence and a receipt from a Harley Street Consultant. When questioned, Daly declined to answer questions on his possession of this correspondence. After a couple of hours, a man called William Goodwin walked into the flat with several bags of groceries and it quickly became clear that he was protecting Daly from arrest and that he was probably being richly rewarded for his efforts.

He was arrested, in his pyjamas, by Tommy Butler, early one morning within four months of the robbery, when one of the men he had paid to look after him, Godfrey Green, grassed him to the Police.

Daly was charged with Armed Robbery and Conspiracy to Rob and, at his trial at Aylesbury Crown Court in April 1964, he appeared together with nine of the other fifteen members of the robbery gang. The case against him was based on the fact that his fingerprints had been found on the Monopoly set found at Leatherslade Farm. During his trial, his QC argued that his fingerprints got onto the Monopoly set before the robbery, when he had played the game with Bruce Reynolds earlier in the year, so that the presence of his fingerprints did not prove that he was involved in the robbery. The judge accepted this and directed the jury in the case that it would be unsafe to convict Daly on the evidence available, so that Daly became the only member of the gang to be acquitted of the crime.

Upon his acquittal, Daly was devastated to discover that he had been deceived by the men that he had trusted to look after his share of the proceeds and that he had been left penniless. He cut his contacts with the criminal fraternity and moved to Launceston in Cornwall, where he would remain for the rest of his life. He became a dustman and street cleaner for the city council, working until he reached the age of 70. After his retirement he continued to do odd cleaning jobs, and became known locally as 'Gentleman John'.

Jimmy White

In his 1978 book *The Train Robbers*, Piers Paul Read described Jimmy White as being '... a solitary thief, not known to work with either firm, he should have had a good chance of remaining undetected altogether, yet he was known to be one of the Train Robbers almost at once – first by other criminals and then by the police'.

White had another advantage. He was a wartime paratrooper and a veteran of the Battle of Arnhem. He was said to have had 'a remarkable ability to be invisible, to merge with his surroundings, and to become the ultimate Mr Nobody.' At the time of the Great Train Robbery he had already been on the run from the Police for ten years, so it can have come as little surprise that he managed to avoid arrest for another three years after the robbery.

But White was an unlucky thief. During his three years on the run after the robbery he was taken advantage of by, or let down by, friends and associates. His flat was broken into by a group of men purporting to be from the Flying Squad, who took a brief case containing £8,500. He was unlucky when Brian Field's relatives dumped luggage containing £100,000 only a mile from a site where White had bought a caravan and hidden £30,000 in the panelling, so that Police enquiries led them to White's caravan and to finding his money.

Finally, he was recognised by one of his new friends from photographs in a newspaper as the wanted train robber that he was, and on 4 April 1966, DCS Tommy Butler received information from an anonymous informant that Jimmy White was living in Littlestone in Kent under the name of Bob Lane and was employed in renovating boats. The caller was unable to answer Butler's specific questions relating to White's address in Littlestone or the registration numbers of either the Land Rover or the private car that he used. He told Butler that he frequently visited Littlestone for fishing and that he could get the information that Butler required on his next visit to Littlestone, which was due to be on 16 April 1966.

As the call ended, Butler despatched two officers to Littlestone to see what was happening, but as soon as they arrived there the officers realised that their presence had doubled the town's population and could not possibly go unnoticed, so they immediately returned to New Scotland Yard. On 12 April 1966 the same informant called Butler again and supplied White's address as being Flat 4 Claverley Mansions and told Butler that since his previous call he had visited the premises at White's request, in order to take a drink with him. He then supplied Butler with the registration numbers of the vehicles that White was using. On 18 April 1966, Butler received a call from Kent Police supplying the same address for White and confirming many of the details supplied by the first informant.

Butler again arranged to send two officers to Littlestone to arrest White on 21 April 1963. They found him at his flat with his wife, Sheree, and baby son, Stephen. They conveyed him to Hammersmith Police Station in West London where, after being interviewed, he was conveyed to Aylesbury Police Station and charged with Armed Robbery and Conspiracy to Rob. White faced evidence that his palm mark had been found on a post-robbery dated copy of *The Oxford Times*, which was found hidden inside a mailbag at Leatherslade Farm.

In June 1966 White appeared before Mr Justice Nield at Leicester Assizes and was sentenced to a total of 18 years imprisonment, considerably less than the 30 years awarded to the other principal offenders. Passions had calmed and the public fever for justice had passed. Despite having never left England following the robbery, he had only £8,000 to hand back to the Police when he was arrested, the rest having gone long ago.

Buster Edwards

On 16 September 1966 Buster Edwards returned to England, from Mexico where he had fled after the robbery, and gave himself up to the newly-promoted Detective Superintendent Frank Williams at the Prince of Wales Public House in Southwark. The arrest was part of a deal that Williams had agreed with Edwards' friend and colleague, Freddie Foreman, but which Williams had not disclosed to DCS Butler. Edwards' money had run out and he really had no other options.

Edwards faced evidence that his fingerprints had been found on a Barclays Bank money wrapper from their Pwllheli Branch that was found at the farm and a left hand print which was found on one of the green (khaki) Land Rovers used in the robbery.

He was charged with Armed Robbery and Conspiracy to Rob and appeared at Nottingham Assizes on 8 and 9 December 1966. At his trial he was sentenced to a total of 15 years imprisonment. He then spent the next nine years in gaol before his early release in 1975.

Once released, Edwards went back to his original job of floristry, and opened up a flower stall outside Waterloo Station. He gave many interviews about the robbery and persuaded the writer Piers Paul Read to add into his 1978 book *The Train Robbers* that the great robbery was in fact led by a German commando called Otto Skorzeny, and that Edwards himself had coshed Jack Mills. Once the book was published, Edwards retracted both of these claims.

Edwards battled with depression and had a severe drink problem. In 1994, at the age of 63, he was found hung in a garage near his flower stall. At his funeral there were two flower wreaths in the shape of trains. In 1988, singer Phil Collins played the role of Buster Edwards in the film *Buster*, which was based on the Great Train Robbery.

Bruce Richard Reynolds

Following the robbery, Reynolds laid low in London, moving between addresses in Croydon, Battersea, Clapham and Belgravia. On one occasion in December 1963, he was found in a first floor flat in Handcroft Road in West Croydon in Surrey, by Police officers investigating the presence of a ladder propped up against an open window. Presumably the ladder had been left in case Police came to arrest Reynolds and he needed to make a speedy getaway. The officers suspected that a burglary was occurring or had occurred at the first floor flat.

The officers called at the flat, where Mrs Reynolds answered the door, and Mr Reynolds was found naked in the bedroom, claiming to be indulging in illicit sex with the lady of the house. The embarrassed police officers made a hasty exit, without recognising Reynolds, despite all the press publicity in the case. By the time that the officers realised their mistake and returned to the address two days later, the Reynolds had fled.

Upon hearing of the sentences handed down to the members of the gang who had been caught, Reynolds fled the country and took his family to Mexico. They later moved to Montreal in Canada, where Charlie Wilson had also fled. Eventually returning to England under the name Keith Hiller, Reynolds and his family settled down at Villa Cap Martin in Braddons Hill Road East, Torquay, Cornwall.

However, the temptation to contact old friends in London eventually led to calls to his family being traced and Reynolds being tracked down. The main evidence against Reynolds was his fingerprints on two Monopoly tokens and a Heinz Tomato Ketchup bottle found at the farm.

One morning in November 1969, Reynolds was awoken from his bed before 7 am by his son Nick, reporting that the doorbell was ringing. Reynolds sent his son downstairs with instructions to answer the door, only to find Tommy Butler in his bedroom, in the company of several burly uniformed officers.

He was charged with Armed Robbery and Conspiracy to Rob and on 14 January 1969 he appeared before Buckinghamshire Assizes at Aylesbury, where he pleaded guilty and was sentenced to a total of 25 years imprisonment. He was released in 1978. Incarcerated again in the 1980s for drug offences, Reynolds found it hard to find work and later admitted that he had became an old crook living on hand-outs from other old crooks. In an effort to generate income, Reynolds wrote his autobiography *The Autobiography of a Thief* and contributed to press, television and film projects based on the Great Train Robbery. Bruce

Reynolds died in his sleep on 28 February 2013 aged 81, following a short illness.

Summary
Towards the end of 1963, there was a review of the case so far. A total of 1,700 exhibits had been prepared and 2,350 statements taken. Nine of the robbers had been arrested and there was no immediate prospect of any further arrests; the time was right to set a date for the trial. The date fixed for the trial was 20 January 1964.

There was more debate about the venue. Both sides realised that it was easier to 'nobble' London juries, so the Old Bailey was out. Aylesbury Assize Court was nowhere near large enough for the crowds felt likely to attend, so the Council Chamber in Aylesbury was adapted for use.

The trial at Aylesbury Crown Court in April 1964 was the end of the first stage of the enquiry into the Great Train Robbery, as twelve convicted men were sentenced to a total of 307 years imprisonment, with seven of the men receiving terms of 30 years, the second longest in modern British criminal history.

Mr Justice Edmund Davies managed to express his feelings about the crime and communicate his sentencing decisions to all twelve of the defendants in just thirty-two minutes. He told one of the convicts that he proposed to do all in his power to ensure that the mail robbery would be the last of its kind.

That was that. The twelve heavily guarded men were driven off to Aylesbury prison to be 'split up' and sent to prisons dotted about the country. Crowds packed the market square outside to watch them go. 'I'm half sorry really,' said one woman. 'We were beginning to feel they belonged to the town.'

By the end of the investigation police officers had taken 2,350 statements from witnesses, which all needed to be written down, typed up, cross referenced and filed; taken possession of more than 1,700 exhibits which all needed to be identified and listed; and written more than 2,000 reports to senior officers and for onward transmission to outside agencies. Detective Superintendent Gerald McArthur and Detective Sergeant Jack Pritchard ran this office and were assisted by no less than fourteen police officers and ten typists.

CHAPTER SEVEN

Nowadays

(This chapter discusses the ways in which the investigation of a similar crime today would vary from the original investigation half a century ago)

Today, when a major incident occurs, police officers attend the scene and report back the support and assistance that they require, so that arrangements can be made to meet their needs. A modern police service has a range of specially trained officers and special equipment that are constantly available to attend the location of any incident, and other emergency services such as the Fire Brigade, Ambulance Service, Coastguard, Army, Navy and Air Force may be called upon as necessary.

Most of us have seen traffic officers, firearms officers, doctors, forensic scientists, fingerprint experts, photographers as well as environmental scientists, local authority highways experts, social workers, care workers and even police and ambulance helicopters at the scene of an incident. As the scope of the enquiry expands, more and more specialists are summoned to the scene, where they meet increasingly senior police officers, summoned to take responsibility for the increasing state activity and public expenditure.

Access may be limited to areas and roads closed. When the bomb went off at Harrods in Knightsbridge in December 1984, the Police closed off an area four miles square, or to put it another way, a radius of roughly two miles from the detonation. This area was kept secure for three to four days as the streets were forensically swept to find every particle from the bomb, so that it might be re-constructed, and any other useful evidence gathered.

Since the 1970s, most police forces have maintained squads of officers who are employed at the force headquarters rather than at police stations and who they keep in reserve, and are not deployed on regular policing but on flexible operations that they can easily drop in order to be at the scene of any major incident within fifteen minutes. In the Metropolitan Police, this unit was originally called the Special Patrol Group (SPG), but in 1980 they were re-organised into the Territorial Support Group (TSG). These officers possess their own transport, special equipment and special training as well as providing the numbers of officers required for tasks such as manning a cordon, which are manpower intensive, and are a great asset at any incident.

The presence of large numbers of officers at a scene of an incident requires that logistical arrangements be made to feed and water them (with mobile cooking facilities, hundreds of catering staff and plenty of food supplies) and to provide toilet facilities for them. Considerable lighting arrangements will be required for the officers to work the scene and for the catering area.

Initially, the investigation of all crimes rests with the local police division based at the local police station. Most divisions have a Criminal Investigation Department (CID) managed by an officer of the rank of Detective Chief Inspector (DCI), a rank at which officers are frequently entrusted with investigating murders, so they are capable of investigating most crimes. Certain crimes, which are considered to require particular skills, knowledge or experience are dealt with by specialist squads based at the local force headquarters, such as the Flying Squad in the Metropolitan Police, which focuses on armed robbery.

The biggest and most serious crimes are now investigated by an officer of the rank of Commander in the Metropolitan Police, which is equivalent to the rank of Assistant Chief Constable in County police forces. Officers above this rank are considered managers and do not investigate crimes, although many of them have done so during their careers.

The next management decision is the size and quality of the initial response, so that the number of officers required to deal with it may be calculated and a decision made whether to authorise large numbers of officers to be retained on duty for long periods of time, which may have a substantial effect on police and public service budgets.

At the time of the Great Train Robbery, Cheddington came under the control of Buckinghamshire Constabulary and the Chief Constable of Buckinghamshire Constabulary, Brigadier Cheney, decided that he could not justify the manpower or overtime that his officers on the enquiry were requesting. As a result, by the time the forensic scientists arrived at the scene of the robbery at daylight on the day of the robbery, British Rail had removed the train engine back to its base in Crewe, thereby obliterating all the forensic evidence such as Jack Mills' blood and hair, and all the robbers' fingerprints as well as any hope of ever finding out who had struck Mills over the head, a key fact of the robbery. There were also insufficient officers to control sightseers at the scene of the robbery, so that groups of young children had been able to climb all over the HVP carriage, the actual scene of the robbery, and obliterate all forensic evidence and fingerprints there.

These were primary lines of enquiry and losing them could have proved fatal to the enquiry, if the robbers had decided to make a dash for London and set fire to the getaway cars, rather than hideaway at the farm. The presence of the robbers' fingerprints at the farm, proved little of real evidential value, compared with any fingerprints that had been found in the HVP or in the engine of the train, where the actual robbery occurred.

There comes a time in any incident in which the enquiry is transferred from the place where it happened to the local police station. This usually happens at some time between the first and fourth day of the enquiry. There is now an opportunity to review the scope of the investigation as a result of the information now available and adjust the number of officers engaged on the enquiry and the facilities available to them, such as office space, transport, computers, etc.

In 1963, Tommy Butler decided that he needed only six officers in order to investigate the Great Train Robbery. Many officers were surprised with how small this number was, even in 1963, but Tommy Butler saw security as a prime requirement and wanted to limit possible leaks of information and ensure that, should those leaks occur, then he could identify the officer or officers responsible. He was acutely aware that he had selected 'the best informed detective in London' in Frank Williams and that the other squad members were probably the runners up in that contest and that, whilst he wanted these officers out on the streets talking to every informant in town, he did not want any whispers about the direction and progress of the investigation going back in the other direction in return.

Butler instructed his officers to get out onto the streets and meet people, to talk to criminals, informants and anybody else who may be able to assist the enquiry. He told them to search premises where it was felt that the robbers or the loot might be, or where useful information might be found, so that crime in London came to an almost standstill after the Robbery, as criminals felt that they and their activities were under close scrutiny. None of these tasks would be seen as essential to the enquiry today.

Today, large major enquiries, such as the investigation of the Harrods Bombing in December 1984, draw in almost the entire available CID workforce so that the enquiry team would be closer to six hundred officers. The reason for this is that there is a focus on blame and accountability. If the police fail to make an arrest it is seen that it must be somebody's fault and that person must lose their job. Either the chief of police failed to allocate the necessary resources or the detective in charge failed to follow up every line of enquiry. One of them should expect to lose his or her job as a result of the failure to achieve a conviction. In order to decide which one of them is at fault every action undertaken by the enquiry team, together with the result of that action, must be documented. Every strategic decision made during the enquiry must be documented, timed and signed, so there is evidence to prove just exactly who was responsible for the failure.

When Hatherill selected Butler to lead the enquiry into the Great Train Robbery, he is extremely unlikely to have considered the possibility that in three months' time, if arrests were not forthcoming, that he might have to replace Butler with another senior detective, who would need to catch up with the work already completed, or that he would need to appoint another senior detective to review the investigation and propose lines of enquiry that had been overlooked, as his modern counterpart would now.

The Yorkshire Ripper Enquiry, based in West Yorkshire but covering all parts of Yorkshire, as well as much of Lancashire, was a watershed in criminal investigation and led to the introduction of a structured format that would allow for a number of Police Forces to investigate crimes, combine their investigations, split their enquiries, appoint new senior investigating officers and allow for management decisions to be recorded so that they could later be reviewed and evaluated by even more senior officers, the Independent Police Complaints Commission (IPCC) , Police Commissioners, the Home Office and the Courts.

Visitors to the Yorkshire Ripper enquiry report their surprise at seeing rooms filled with boxes of documents, waiting to be added to the card carousels that were used to index the names of those stopped, searched, interviewed, etc. Eventually, Peter Sutcliffe was arrested not as a result of a computer identifying a trend and printing out an instruction to arrest him (although his name appeared six times in the enquiry) but as a result of good old fashioned police work by two uniformed patrol officers. Despite the arrest of Sutcliffe, and his confessions so that no doubt remained as to his guilt, the investigation had to continue so that all the documents were input and officers were able to satisfy the court about issues that were raised during the trial.

As a result of the debacle in the Yorkshire Ripper Enquiry, which resulted from an enquiry covering an unprecedented number of crimes over an unprecedented number of force areas, the Home Office decided to commission the HOLMES Project, or the Home Office Large Major Enquiry Project, so that in future all enquiries could follow the same format, the same structure, the same forms and the same administration and management. Inspirational geniuses like Tommy Butler would be of limited use nowadays.

Today there is no room for detectives like Tommy Butler, who rely on inspiration, 'gut-feeling' and the 'word on the street' rather than the perspiration of making sure that every address receives a visit and every resident is spoken to and all the results are collated and inputted into the computer system. However all this paperwork has created its own problems with storage, retention, access, etc.

In 1963, Tommy Butler carried a notebook in his inside jacket pocket. Few people ever saw it and nobody ever got to read it. It contained the list of names of people that he considered to be suspects for the Robbery. It was so secret that Frank Williams, his deputy, had to prepare his own list of suspects and his frequent requests to compare the two lists were constantly rejected by Butler. If Butler had had his way his notebook in his pocket would probably have been the only piece of paper used by the investigators. You don't want to keep much paper if you are trying to keep secrets as other people will read the files and check the bins.

Tommy Butler and his team were selected because they were the very best detectives in the country, possibly in the world. They had the trust of the Prime Minister, the Home Secretary, the Commissioner, the Assistant Commissioner (Crime) and his deputy, Hatherill. And they wanted Butler's squad out on the streets, solving crime, not sitting in a police canteen writing reports.

Today civil liberties have a greater priority and officers have to make comprehensive reports on every individual they speak to, and further reports if they then go on to search those individuals and then more reports if they search their vehicles and even more reports if they search their premises. Somebody is then required to collate and index all this documentation and having done that, it might as well be inputted into computers so that it can later be traced if required. But even after the documents have been inputted into the computer system, it is not permitted to destroy them and instead they have to be collated and stored in a system where they can be later accessed if required at court or as part of some review of the investigation. Now the administration team is larger than the investigating team.

The investigation team needs to be based near the scene of the enquiry, as that is where they will be working. They also need to be near the administration team because they have to work closely with them. All these people need offices, telephones, computers, scanners, printers and the usual office equipment. All this will have to be set up specially as it has probably never been required at this place before and will probably never be required there again.

Nowadays, senior police officers recognise the necessity to recover large sums of stolen cash and negotiables which can be used to undermine currency, fund terrorism, arrange executions, etc. The experience of the Brink's-MAT Robbery at Heathrow Airport in November 1983, in which £26 million of gold bullion was stolen, showed how even the largest sums may be cleverly invested in projects such as the Canary Wharf Development, so as to become even greater sums. The partnerships that the robbers formed with financial experts at that time persist to this day. The negotiations, however, led to the violent deaths of many of those involved, such as Charlie Wilson, the Great Train Robber, who was tasked with investing some of the proceeds from Brink's-MAT, but who managed to lose £3 million for the Brink's-MAT team and was shot and killed on his doorstep in Spain as a lesson to others. In his book, Wensley Clarkson links sixteen deaths with the Brink's-MAT job. Today a second investigating team would be set up to recover the stolen money.

In 1964, twelve months after the Robbery, Frank Williams realised that all but three of the suspects for the Robbery were convicted and serving prison sentences, but that less than £350,000 of the proceeds of the crime had been recovered. Keen to deprive the Robbers of the benefits that the money would provide, either for those still at large or for those who were serving but who would eventually be released, Williams started to negotiate for the return of the money. But when he started to achieve results, Butler, Millen and Hatherill offered him no encouragement or support and rather saw that as the role of the insurance loss adjusters. In fact, when Williams told Butler that he was popping out to collect £50,000 that the Robbers had promised to leave in a telephone box relatively close to Scotland Yard, Butler ordered him back to his desk, preferring to leave this substantial sum of money where it could be stolen again rather than spend a few minutes sweeping it up.

Undeterred, Williams continued to negotiate for the return of the proceeds of the Robbery, but as a result his superiors questioned his honesty and loyalty and he, despite several promotions, was deprived of the ultimate prize that he sought, that of being appointed to be Detective Chief Superintendent of the Flying Squad, Butler's job.

Clearly, recent governments have reflected society's concerns by introducing safeguards and accountability in order to protect civil liberties and impose accountability on those officers appointed to direct police forces and lead major enquiries. These measures mean that the number of officers required to conduct an investigation has increased dramatically. The amount of equipment required has similarly increased and these increases have been reflected in the costs of a criminal investigation.

Perhaps more worryingly, it has pushed investigating officers to focus excessively on any subsequent reviews of the investigation and the investigation of any complaints made about it, and to adopt an increasingly mechanical approach to enquiries instead of their preferred intuitive style.

CHAPTER EIGHT

The Trial

It was the television personality Sir David Frost who with Sir Anthony Jay wrote, 'A broad definition of crime in England is that it is any lower class activity that is displeasing to the upper classes.' (*To England with Love*)

This is, to an extent, inevitable. Those who have property do not have to steal it from others. Those who own mansions where they can eat, drink and socialise will ask their guests to leave rather than use violence on them; the masses crammed into the local public house have only one way to resolve their problems.

Laws are written in Parliament, where members are drawn from the upper classes. Common Law was set down by the high echelons of the legal profession, where members were drawn from among the high social classes of middle aged, white, Anglo Saxon males.

The law has always been enforced by the same legal profession. They wore chalk wigs and ancient gowns. They sat in aging courts and when somebody was convicted and sentenced to imprisonment they were sent to a decaying building with high walls where the prisoners were required to slop-out every morning.

When, towards the end of 1963, there was a general consensus among the Police, the Prison Service, the Home Office and the Lord Chancellor's Department, which ran the courts, that it was about time to start thinking about arranging for those already charged in connection with the Great Train Robbery, to stand trial, it was this class-based system into which the defendants were pitched.

The Police recognised that they had ten of the robbers in custody, but that they had failed to identify three of the robbers and that whilst they had published the identity and photographs of three suspects, Bruce Reynolds, Buster Edwards and Jimmy White, they were not close to arresting them. These ten men were all in prison custody awaiting their trial, having been recognised by the courts as flight risks in view of the substantial prison sentences that they faced and the exceptionally large amount of money that they had in their possession.

The Government realised that the case of the Great Train Robbers presented them with unprecedented problems. The robbers were entitled to a public trial where all the witnesses against them had to be presented as well as all the exhibits. Each robber had the right to be represented by all the solicitors and barristers that they required. There was a considerable public interest in the case and security was a major concern, so large numbers of uniformed and plain clothes detectives would be required.

Clearly, a very large building would be required for the trial, much larger than the local Crown Court building at Aylesbury. The Defence Counsel saw the search for a larger venue as the perfect opportunity to press for the trial to be moved to the Central Criminal Court, sitting at the Old Bailey in London. As the senior court for hearing criminal cases in England and Wales, it clearly had jurisdiction to hear the case, and as the venue for many of the largest and most important trials in the country, it also had the facilities to handle such trials. But it was the opportunity to influence, or even tamper, with the jury that the defendants sought.

The Government decided to invest a considerable amount of money to convert Aylesbury Council Chamber into a temporary annex to Aylesbury Crown Court, so that the trial could remain in Aylesbury, but more importantly, the jurors could be selected from the local Aylesbury population.

Five and a half months after the robbery, on Monday 20 January 1964, thirteen of the robbers and seven receivers appeared at Aylesbury Rural District Council Chamber, which had been made an annex of Aylesbury Assizes. After two hours of frantic activity, at 10.30 am, the usher called those present to stand for the entry of the judge, Mr Justice Edmund Davies.

Once the lawyers had introduced themselves to the judge and identified their clients to him, the clerk of the court stood and read the charges to the prisoners and recorded their pleas. Roger Cordrey was first up and pleaded guilty to Conspiracy to Rob and three charges of Receiving Stolen Money, the proceeds of the robbery, but not guilty to involvement in the robbery. The other defendants denied everything alleged against them.

The judge then adjourned the case against all those accused of Receiving Stolen Goods, effectively splitting the indictment of the Receivers from those accused of the Robbery. Then, following the prosecuting counsel's acceptance of Cordrey's plea of not guilty to the charge of Robbery, the judge instructed that Cordrey be put down until the end of the trial of the other defendants, when he would re-join them for sentencing.

This left the twelve remaining Robbers, sitting in two rows of six, Boal, Wilson, Biggs, Wisbey, Welch and Hussey sitting in the front row and Daly, James, Goody, Brian Field, Lennie Field and Wheater in the back row. Several of the defendants were wearing expensive clothing, which raised eyebrows in a provincial town and caused questions to be asked as to how men who were unemployed or claiming to be employed in unskilled manual jobs, could afford such items.

Mr Ivor Richard, representing Brian Field, then raised a point of law with the judge. He reported that Brian's wife, Karin Field, had been approached by an unknown man making an offer to ensure that he was acquitted if she paid him £3,000. The judge asked for Mrs Field to be brought before the court, but was told by Mr Richard that she had 'Gone shopping'. When Mr Richard told the judge that the allegation had been reported to Tommy Butler, the judge summoned him and questioned him about the matter. Butler reported that he had arranged with Mrs Field for her to meet the man at Reading Station and had intercepted him there and interviewed him. Butler expressed the view that the man was attempting to climb the criminal ladder, rather than attempting to influence the result of the trial. Twenty minutes later, Karin Field was brought before the court and was questioned by the judge. As a result of what he was told, the judge decided that no further action was required and announced that he would be moving on.

Twelve Buckinghamshire men were then selected to form the jury:

George Plested
William J. Grant
Arthur Edward Greedy
Norman Mace

Richard Thomas Tadman
Terrance Addy
Frederick Freeman
Williams Mullins
George Edward Pargeter
Alexander Sinclair Watt
Ernest F.M. Smith
Leonard Thane

They were then sworn in.

The judge then made his introductory comments to the court and then Mr Arthur James QC, the leading Counsel for the Prosecution, made his opening speech, which took ten hours over two days.

For the next thirteen days hundreds of witnesses came, gave their evidence and went away again. Then as Detective Sergeant Stanley Davies of Bournemouth CID gave his evidence, Bill Boal jumped to his feet and shouted, 'It's a lie, a deliberate lie!' His barrister, Mr Sime QC, jumped to his feet to raise a point of law. As soon as the jury had retired from the courtroom, he went on to explain to the court that he wished to draw the court's attention to his client's allegation that the officer had 'verballed' him and that he had failed to caution his client in accordance with Judges' Rules. The judge told Mr Sime that he understood the points that he was making, but that he would allow the officer's evidence to go to the jury.

Two days later when Detective Sergeant John Swain was giving evidence of searching Gordon Goody's address at 6 Commonside in Putney, he was asked by Goody's Counsel, Mr Sebag Shaw QC, whether he possessed a search warrant at the time. Swain admitted that he did not. After a heated exchange, he finally admitted that he had told Mrs Goody that he held a search warrant. The judge, clearly upset, said, 'See it never happens again.' And Mr Shaw went on to say, 'There was no reason to search the house at that stage. That was why there was no warrant.'

Later Detective Chief Inspector Peter Vibart gave evidence of questioning Goody in Leicester and admitted that he had not been cautioned before he was questioned. Mr Shaw was soon on his feet complaining that the officer had failed to comply with Judges' Rules. Again the judge ruled that he would allow the evidence to go before the jury. Clearly, the pressure to secure a result had caused the police to cut corners.

On Thursday 30 January, the judge announced to the court that he had received an anonymous letter instructing him as to the way that he should conduct his duties during the trial. He did not state in which way he had been instructed to act, in favour of the prosecution or the defence, or whether any consequences had been set down if he failed to comply with the instructions. He simply warned others considering writing or sending similar messages as to the consequences of so doing.

On Friday 31 January, Mr Michael Argyle QC for Lennie Field raised a point of law as Detective Inspector Harry Tappin was giving evidence of Tommy Butler interviewing Field. As the jury retired, Mr Argyle pointed out that Butler had not cautioned Field and had therefore breached Judges' Rules. After considering the matter, the judge announced that he would allow the oral evidence given by DI Tappin to go before the jury, but that he would withhold the written statement made by Field.

On Wednesday 5 February Dr Ian Holden, the forensic scientist, was called to the stand to give evidence in relation to the yellow paint found on property belonging to Bill Boal and Gordon Goody. Counsel for both men strenuously attacked the evidence, but throughout the day Holden showed why he was considered such an excellent expert witness. Eventually the judge challenged Mr Shaw for Goody as to whether he was accusing the witness of lying. This is important because if an accused alleges that a prosecution witness is lying, then the usual bar to revealing the prisoner's criminal history is lifted as the need for the jury to evaluate whether to believe the accused or the witness is considered more important than concealing the prisoner's criminal history. Mr Shaw told the judge that he did not wish to make any allegations, and Goody's criminal history therefore remained hidden from the jury.

On Thursday 6 February, Detective Inspector Basil Morris of Surrey Police was called to give evidence relating to his interview with Ronnie Biggs days after the robbery. He related how he had asked Biggs whether he knew Bruce Reynolds and stated that Biggs said, 'I knew Reynolds some years ago. We did time together.' At this the judge twitched and looked at Biggs' Counsel, Mr Wilfred Fordham, but Fordham decided to allow Morris to finish his evidence before rising to tell the judge that he wished to make a point of law. Once the jury had left the court, Mr Fordham pointed out to the judge that DI Morris had, albeit indirectly, told the jury that Biggs had a previous conviction. The judge was compelled to agree and Biggs was told that he was being discharged and that another trial would be arranged in due course. (This is a bad mistake, especially for an officer of this rank and experience, and Morris got in serious trouble for it.)

The Prosecution closed their case on Tuesday 11 February and there followed a string of submissions from the Defence barristers. The first submission was made by Mr Walter Raeburn QC on behalf of Daly. He submitted that his client had no case to answer as his fingerprints were found on a Monopoly board that was not always at the farm and that, although his client had been unwise to go into hiding when the police were looking for him, this proved nothing.

After listening carefully to all the submissions, the judge recalled the jury and announced that he was rejecting all of the submissions except for the one made on behalf of Daly and that he had decided, on a point of law, to direct the jury to acquit Daly as it would be unsafe to convict him on the evidence placed before the court. Mr Fordham then asked that his client's legal expenses be paid from public funds. The judge immediately refused this application, indicating where he felt the responsibility lay for his client being charged.

Daly was immediately released from court to face the press and was then given a lift back to Aylesbury Prison to pick up his personal property, and return to his wife who had given birth to their son in his absence. The most damning evidence against Daly is just how he afforded the top-flight legal team that got him acquitted when he had not worked for so long and had previously only held unskilled positions.

It was now the opportunity for the defence and the first up was Bill Boal. Boal claimed that he was no way involved in the robbery. Of course, he had to explain how he came to be in Bournemouth with Roger Cordrey who had pleaded guilty to Conspiracy to Rob and being found in possession of £141,000. His greatest problem was that he needed to call Cordrey to give evidence on his behalf but that Cordrey could not give evidence that Boal was innocent without facing prosecution questions about the guilt or innocence of each of the other robbers, and Wilson had made it clear what he would do to anyone who talked to the police about the robbery. Boal was left to give evidence on his own behalf and deny any involvement in the robbery. He produced a National Insurance cheque for £8 that he had cashed on the day of the robbery and had to hope for a positive result from the jury.

Jim Hussey, Bob Welch and Tommy Wisbey all gave the court the same story: that they had met up for a drink with a man called Dark Ronnie at Hussey's house in Camberwell on Saturday 10 August. He had sought their assistance to take a lorry load of fruit and vegetables down the A40 and that he had stopped at a farm on the way. They felt that this farm must have been Leatherslade Farm and that this was how their fingerprints came to be found on items from the farm. The prosecution placed an advertisement in *The Evening Standard* seeking to trace Dark Ronnie and were contacted by a Mr Ronald Darke who attended court and confirmed the statements made by the three defendants. It was now a matter of who the jury believed.

Roy James' defence revolved around the fact that he was found in possession of £12,000 of brand new banknotes issued after the robbery – so clearly not the proceeds of the robbery (but possibly the laundered proceeds of the robbery?). He then called two taxi drivers who took him to a club the evening before the robbery and took him home after the time of the robbery. His story lost credibility when the prosecution gained an admission that one of the taxi drivers had visited him seventeen times whilst he was on remand at Aylesbury Prison and was therefore a close friend.

Charlie Wilson declined to give evidence in his own defence, so enhancing his reputation during the trial as 'the silent man'. Ironically, this meant that the jury were left with the words that the press had reported that he made to the police when he was arrested: 'I don't see how you can make it without the poppy [money] and you won't find that.' Despite the advice of lawyers, most people find it difficult to believe that an innocent man will not speak in his own defence.

The night before Gordon Goody got to deliver his defence a *Daily Express* reporter, Ian Buchan, was interviewed by Police for the entire night. He eventually admitted agreeing to give Goody a false alibi in exchange for an exclusive interview. The next morning Goody told the court how he had twice appeared at court charged with the BOAC Heathrow Robbery and twice been acquitted. He told the court that the Police hated him and would do anything to convict him.

On Monday 24 February, Brian Field set out his defence through his barrister. He called several character witnesses and then appeared relaxed and confident as he gave evidence on his own behalf. He told the court that he did own the bags found loaded with cash in Dorking Woods, but that they had been stolen from his office, probably by one of his robber clients. It was an amusing interlude in a rather stressful case.

On Friday 28 February it was the turn of Leonard Field to hear the evidence against him. When he had signed the documents for the purchase of Leatherslade Farm, he had been told that all he had to do was keep away from their office and that he would be handsomely rewarded. Now he realised that Wheater and Brian Field had documented his involvement in the robbery to such an extent that he had no way out.

The expert testimony given by Dr Holden in relation to the yellow paint found on Gordon Goody's shoes and in the pocket of Bill Boal had not been rebutted by an expert called on behalf of the defence by the time that the defence had run out of witnesses and were otherwise ready to make their closing speeches.

Originally a Dr Grant, the proprietor of Hehner and Cox (Consulting Chemists) had been retained to perform this role, but he had been called away to Pakistan on urgent business before the trial started and had not returned by the time that all the other defence evidence had been heard, so that arrangements had to be made for two of his staff to replace him. Mr Cecil Hancorn Robins and Mr Douglas Nicholas held only

Bachelor's degrees (as against Holden's doctorate) and had no experience giving expert witness in court, so the jury probably only understood a small proportion of the evidence that they gave over the next week.

Between Tuesday 10 and Saturday 14 March the best barristers in English criminal law reviewed the evidence that the jury had heard and explained why they thought that it should either persuade the jury to convict or acquit the defendants. Finally, on Monday 16 March the judge was due to set out the law for them, before sending the jury out to consider their verdict. But before he was able to do so, there was just one more final twist.

Mr Arthur James QC, for the Crown, rose to make a point of law and went on to explain to the judge that one of the jurors had visited his local police station over the weekend to explain that he had been approached about accepting money in order to influence his verdict. Having already received a note on the matter, the judge was not surprised. He congratulated juror number 6, Mr Terrance Addy, from Chalfont St Giles, on behaving with perfect rectitude and asked him to go with Malcolm Fewtrell, the clerk of the court and the shorthand writer to a side room where he could set out the facts to the officer so that a decision could be made as to whether an offence of Embracery (illegally and corruptly influencing a jury) had occurred.

Twenty minutes later the court re-convened and the statement taken from Mr Addy was presented to the judge, who reminded the jury of the warning that he had given them at the start of the trial. Each defence barrister then rose to his feet to address the judge, so that he could distance his client from any attempt to influence the jury and to exploit.

Uniquely, the judge ended his summing up by telling the jury about what they would need to bring with them for the time that they were sequestered, the way that they would be required to behave whilst they were sequestered and that he had instructed the police to provide all reasonable security measures to protect their families in their absence.

The task of delivering a verdict in a criminal trial in England and Wales has, since AD 1168 AD, rested with the jury. In 1964 juries were selected from among the men living in the area of the court and no special educational qualifications were required for the role. This means that the law is written by lawyers, lawyers (including the judge) explain the law to the jury, and lawyers for the prosecution and defence highlight different aspects of the evidence and different aspects of the law that they feel should direct the jury either to convict or acquit the defendants.

The problem with this is that there is seldom a lawyer (or anybody with any knowledge or experience of the law) on the jury, so that much of what the jury have been told over the weeks of the trial is beyond them, so that instead of deciding the case on its legal merits, they may allow themselves to be swayed by prejudices such as the age, colour, race, gender, gender-orientation or behaviour of the defendants, or possibly by some affiliation with the witnesses or defendants, such as political or masonic ones, or, as was alleged on several occasions during the trial of those accused of involvement in the Great Train Robbery, by the financial and threatening interventions of friends of the defendants.

So it was that on Monday 23 March twelve jurors filed out of Aylesbury Rural District Council chamber carrying their overnight bags and bundles of statements and exhibits on their way to Grange Youth Club in Aylesbury, where they would be staying until they reached a verdict in respect of each of the charges against each of the defendants, or until they were discharged from doing so by the judge.

The prospect of being away from their families for the forthcoming Easter weekend focused the jury's mind and at 8.15 pm on Wednesday 25 March they announced that they had reached unanimous verdicts. It had taken sixty-five hours, which was more than any previous criminal trial in history.

Rather than re-convene the court at 10.00 pm, the judge waited until 10.30 am the next day and the clerk required the jury foreman to announce their verdict on each of the charges against each of the defendants. To each charge of Robbery and Conspiracy to Rob he announced a guilty verdict until the final defendant, John Wheater, was found Not Guilty to the charge of Conspiracy to Rob. Solicitor John Wheater, Clerk Brian Field, and purchaser Lennie Field were then convicted of Conspiracy to Pervert the Course of Justice, before the judge discharged the jury from their duty charges of Receiving Stolen Property against James and Boal, who had already been convicted of more serious charges.

The Judge then thanked the jury for their attention throughout the trial, and their efforts, and sent them home for an early Easter break. After fifty days in court they probably felt that they needed a break.

Any thoughts that any of the outstanding gang members had of surrendering to police, would have been put to one side at the almost one hundred per cent conviction rate achieved in the first trial.

Less than two weeks later, on Wednesday 8 April, Justice Edmund Davies sat at Aylesbury Crown Court to hear the case against Ronald Biggs. The court room, while not large enough for the large number of defendants and lawyers in the main trial, was easily large enough for just one defendant and his legal team. Due to the importance and political significance of the trial, Justice Edmund Davies had probably been struck off from hearing other cases for several weeks so that he could complete the trial and any retrials without interruption. A new jury of nine men and three women was selected to decide the case.

Having already honed their evidence in the original trial, the prosecution closed their case by the close of business on Friday 10 April with only one notable difference from the first trial, when a chastened Detective Inspector Basil Morris gave a varied, inaccurate, but agreed statement that he had admitted that he 'knew Biggs some years ago', but not mentioning the time Biggs and Reynolds shared in prison together.

On Monday 13 April, Biggs went into the witness box to tell the court about a man who had been a close friend for thirteen years who had invited him to 'do a job' with him. Despite being a close friend, the man failed to attend court to give evidence and the story lost most of its value to the jury.

On Tuesday 14 April, the jury adjourned for a brief ninety minute consideration of the evidence, before returning to the court to announce their unanimous verdict on both charges.

On the next day, Wednesday 15 March, Tommy Butler spent the day in the witness box, giving details of the antecedents and previous criminal convictions of the eleven men convicted at the first two trials.

On Thursday 16 March, Justice Edmund Davies sentenced the eleven convicted robbers in thirty minutes, whilst expressing himself freely on his view of their conduct and its consequences. The robbers were taken from court to serve their sentences in separate prisons, away from their co-conspirators. Tommy Butler and Malcolm Fewtrell had both completed their thirty years police service and were now due to retire. Fewtrell immediately submitted his papers to his Chief Constable and promptly left the service to catch up with his retirement. Butler went to see Hatherill to point out that the job was not yet finished, that he still needed to catch Jimmy White, Buster Edwards and Bruce Reynolds and that in view of the results so far, he should be given another year to complete the task. Hatherill had to agree and Butler was allowed to extend his service by twelve months.

Justice Edmund Davies still had the various friends and relatives of the robbers to deal with on the various charges of Receiving Stolen Goods and this was quickly resolved. He then undertook his final task in relation to the case: that of commending a number of the officers involved in the investigation. He commended:

- Detective Superintendent Gerald McArthur and Detective Sergeant John Pritchard, the two Metropolitan Police officers sent to Aylesbury to assist the local police.
- Detective Superintendent Malcolm Fewtrell, the Head of Buckinghamshire Constabulary CID
- Detective Chief Superintendent Tommy Butler and his Flying Squad team under the supervision of Commander George Hatherill, who had conducted the bulk of the investigation and arrested most of the gang.
- Chief Inspector Reginald Ballinger, the uniformed officer, who had managed all the court arrangements throughout the trial.
- Detective Constable Keith Milner and Detective Sergeant William Collins, the two exhibits officers in the case.

The judge went on to explain that he could not hope to name every officer who deserved to be mentioned and asked to be forgiven for any officers that he had not mentioned.

The cases against the Great Train Robbers were listed before the Court of Criminal Appeal at the Royal Courts of Justice in the Strand in the West End of London during the week of Monday 6 July 1964. For convenience the gang was split up over the week. On Monday the cases against Wilson, Biggs and James (as mentioned elsewhere, Wilson did not attend court, preferring instead to escape from prison). On Tuesday it was the turn of Hussey and Wisbey. On Wednesday it was Welch and Goody. All sentences were stoutly upheld with strong comments on the behaviour of the robbers.

On Thursday, John Wheater's sentence was upheld, but Brian Field and Lennie Field had better luck when their sentences were reduced to 5 years imprisonment.

On Monday 13 July Roger Cordrey and Bill Boal appeared before the Court of Appeal. The Court recognised that Bill Boal was much older that the other robbers, and lacked the health and fitness necessary to participate and accordingly allowed his appeal on the charge of Robbery and substituted a conviction for Receiving Stolen Goods, but dismissed his appeal against his conviction for Conspiracy to Rob. Accordingly, his sentence reduced from twenty-four years to fourteen years.

All the defendants applied for leave to appeal to the House of Lords (which pre-dated the Supreme Court), but were told that there was no point of law of general or public interest, and their applications were turned down.

Less than a year after the robbery, justice had been dispensed and the case against the robbers had been closed. There were no further appeals possible and the cell doors had finally closed on the robbers.

Almost exactly a year after the robbery, on 12 August 1964 at 3.15 am, Charlie Wilson was asleep in his cell at Winson Green Prison in Birmingham when he was awoken by a rattling of his cell door. The door opened, three men entered, and one of the men said, 'You're coming out.'

Unsurprisingly, Wilson later claimed not to know these men or what they had planned. He was never likely to admit arranging for them to 'spring' him from prison and paying their wages and expenses as part of some large conspiracy, as this would render him liable to an extended sentence. Instead, Wilson claimed that it was all a great surprise to him and that when he was told that he was coming out, he had said, 'No, I ain't,' and that he only agreed to reluctantly leave his cell, and the prison, when the men produced a revolver and placed him in handcuffs.

His appeal against his 30 year sentence had been heard only a few days earlier and, interestingly, Wilson had refused to attend court to hear the judgement. Most robbers, whether expecting to win or lose their appeal, take the opportunity to enjoy a day out at court in order to escape the tedium of prison life. As might have been reasonably anticipated, none of the robbers who did attend court were returned to the same gaol after the hearing as they had come from. By refusing to attend court for the appeal, Wilson ensured that he was still at Winson Green when the escape committee turned up. A suspicious person might think that he knew more about his visitors and their plans than he was admitting.

Wilson followed the three men out of his cell, down the corridor, past a bound and gagged warder, out of C Wing and into the centre of the prison. They then entered A Wing, passed the bathhouse, went down the stairs and into the prison grounds. To highlight the fact that he was only leaving the prison under duress, Wilson left wearing only a vest.

In order to avoid being seen in the moonlight, the four men kept to the shadows of the buildings and made for the prison walls. They then threw rope ladders over the twenty foot high walls, which they used to scale them, and then to climb down into a builder's yard on the other side. They then crossed another wall so as to run along the canal towpath on the other side and jump into two cars waiting on the road nearby.

After a fifteen minute drive the four men reached a flat on the other side of Birmingham and ran inside. Now everybody relaxed. The gun was put away, the handcuffs were removed and Wilson was given some new clothes to replace the vest that he had left prison wearing. After a couple of days, Wilson's new friends drove him to London and to a flat in Knightsbridge, where he remained for several months, being looked after by a friend who was also a member of the Richardson gang.

Wilson initially hoped that the hue and cry surrounding his escape would soon die away, but as he waited he began to realise that the intensity and scope of the original Flying Squad enquiry would be extended to the attempts to re-capture him and that, whilst it did, he would be unable to see his wife and children. He realised that his only option was to leave the country.

At the end of 1964 he obtained a passport in the name of Ronald Alloway and in March 1965 he took a ferry from Dover to Calais, disguised as a schoolteacher on a hitchhiking holiday. In France he was picked up by one of his friends and driven to the south of France, where in June he was reunited with his wife and youngest daughter.

Eleven months later, on Thursday 8 July 1965, Ronnie Biggs escaped from Wandsworth Prison in South West London. Biggs' wife Charmian had delivered £10,000 to a recently-released inmate from Wandsworth, Paul Seabourne, who made the necessary arrangements.

Seabourne purchased a pantechnicon, cut away the roof and installed a scaffolding tower capable of reaching the height of the prison wall. Then he purchased a rope ladder, an axe and shotguns and hired two friends for £2,500 each, to assist him with the escape. Simultaneously Biggs and his friend, Eric Flowers, arranged to pay £500 each to two prisoners who would assist them inside the prison on the day.

At 3.05 pm the pantechnicon stopped near the prison wall and Seabourne and one of his assistants raised the tower, jumped onto the prison wall, and threw down a rope ladder, whilst the other accomplice pointed his shotgun at the men in the yard below. Biggs and Flower, on an exercise break in the yard below, ran to the wall with two warders chasing after them. The warders were obstructed and jostled by the two paid convicts. In a few minutes Biggs and Flowers climbed up the rope ladder, over the wall, and jumped down onto a mattress in the floor of the pantechnicon. They were then driven away in the two stolen cars through the side streets of London.

Biggs' escape, following less than a year after Wilson's, prompted even greater police action. While Biggs and Flower hid out in Dulwich, 150 police officers, armed with rifles, revolvers and tear gas raided a deserted country house in

Cranleigh in Surrey, and one hundred policemen, together with a Royal Navy helicopter, surrounded Upton House near Poole in Dorset, the English home of Prince Carol of Romania. An anonymous caller had claimed to have seen Biggs hiding in the grounds.

Six weeks after his escape, Biggs moved from Dulwich to Bognor Regis, where Charmian was able to visit him. In October 1965, he was smuggled out of the country to France where, in the Clinique Victor Massein in Paris, he underwent plastic surgery in order to change his appearance. Two months later, on 29 December 1965, he flew from Orly Airport to Australia under the name of Terence Furminger, and six months after that, when he had settled in Adelaide, he was joined by his wife and children.

CHAPTER NINE

The Summary

(A modern summary of what went well and what went badly, both for the Police and the robbers)

A Review of Performance

The Robbers

The Great Train Robbery was exceptionally well planned and the robbers enjoyed excellent good fortunate throughout. Their problems were caused by the fact that the plan was designed, and the gang led, by a committee of four, which made them vulnerable when things went wrong and instant decisions needed to be made.

1. The gang's first mistake was accepting Ronnie Biggs' assurances that his train driver, 'Pops' would be able to move the train. With the months of research that the gang made, it is difficult to understand why they did not put him on a train and test his skills. Using Jack Mills to drive the train solved their immediate problem of moving the train, but meant that the train driver and his assistant were allowed to see the gang's army-style lorry and two Land Rovers. This meant that the robbers could no longer use these vehicles, for fear of detection, and that they were then left with one bicycle between the sixteen of them. Cue the sudden appearance at second-hand car forecourts for miles around of 'cockney blokes in dark glasses buying motors with large bundles of used fivers.'

2. The original plan anticipated a 'take' of up to £1 million, but the gang had been disappointed several times when they had 'opened the box' to find less than half the sum that they expected. If they had really been confident of stealing so much money, they should have made plans for dealing with the money after the robbery.

3. The gang's biggest mistake was in failing to ensure that Brian Field and 'The Dustman' performed the duties for which he had been paid so handsomely. Leatherslade Farm was left crammed with such straightforward clues as fingerprints, the instruction manual for the handcuffs used on the driver, more than 350 empty mailbags, and £628 in unwanted Scottish banknotes (in England, it seems, even thieves don't take those).

The Police

A review of the investigation reveals that there were four serious problems with it:

1. Brigadier Cheney, the Chief Constable of Buckinghamshire Police, restricted overtime from the very start of the enquiry, so that manpower was limited throughout the initial enquiries. This meant that when the Forensic Science Team arrived at daybreak on 8 August 1963, the train engine had already been taken back to Crewe by British Rail and that local children had been allowed to climb around in the HVP carriage so as to obliterate any forensic evidence such as fingerprints.
2. The search for the suspects and their hideout was carried out from the scene to the perimeter, rather than from the perimeter back to the scene.
3. The robbers were allowed to stay at Leatherslade Farm for twenty-seven hours after a member of the public contacted Police in Bedfordshire to report that he suspected that the strange men occupying it were the Great Train Robbers. They were also permitted to tidy it up before they left and it was only due to good fortune by the Police that they were not allowed to burn the place down and totally conceal their identities and conceal the evidence that eventually convicted them.
4. The identities of the robbers and their wives and their photos were circulated on the authority of Commander of the Met CID, George Hatherill, upon the recommendation of Detective Chief Superintendent Ernie Millen, the Head of the Met Flying Squad, a few days after the robbery. This led

to the robbers escaping to all parts of the world and delayed their apprehension by several years.

Why was the train robbed in the first place? The problem was not so much that the security precautions were inadequate, as that there were no precautions at all. The Glasgow-to-London mail train simply trundled through the night picking up bags of used fivers, often left sitting around unattended on station platforms. No police or security guards were on board. The staff on the train had no way of communicating with each other, let alone with the outside world. And just to make it easier, the loot was always carried in the same place: the second carriage from the front. SOMEBODY WAS ALWAYS GOING TO ROB THE TRAIN!

The Robbery in Context

Events 1961 to 1965

1961

7 January – *The Avengers* television series first screened on ITV.

9 January – British authorities announce that they have discovered a large Soviet spy ring in London.

8 March – Edwin Bush is arrested in London for the capital stabbing of Mrs Elsie May Batten. He is the first British criminal identified by the Identikit facial composite system.

13 March – the five members of the Portland Spy Ring go on trial at the Old Bailey accused of passing nuclear secrets to the Soviet Union. Black and white £5 notes cease to be legal tender.

1 May – Betting shops are legalised.

8 May – George Blake is sentenced to 42 years imprisonment for spying, having been found guilty of being a double agent in the pay of the Soviet Union.

4 July – Barclays open their 'No. 1 Computer Centre' in Drummond Street, London, with an EMI mainframe computer, Britain's first bank with an in-house computing centre.

23 August – Police launch a manhunt for the perpetrator of the A6 murder, who shot dead 36-year-old Michael Gregsten and paralysed his mistress Valerie Storie.

17 September – Police arrest over 1,300 protesters in Trafalgar Square during a CND rally.

25 October – The first edition of *Private Eye*, the satirical magazine, is published.

1962

2 January – BBC television broadcasts the first episode of *Z-Cars*, noted as a realistic portrayal of the police.

4 April – James Hanratty is hanged at Bedford Prison for the A6 murder, despite protestations from many people who believed he was innocent, and the late introduction of witnesses who claimed to have seen him in Rhyl, North Wales, on the day of the murder.

2 June – Britain's first legal casino opens in Brighton, Sussex.

11 July – Live television broadcast from the USA to Britain for the first time, via the Telstar satellite and Goonhilly Satellite Earth Station.

5 October – *Dr No*, the first James Bond film, is released, with 32-year-old Edinburgh-born Sean Connery playing the lead, a British Secret Service agent.

24 November – The first episode of influential satire show *That Was The Week That Was* is broadcast on BBC Television.

2–7 December – Severe smog in London causes numerous deaths.

10 December – Britons Francis Crick and Maurice Wilkins, along with American James D. Watson, win the Nobel Prize in Physiology or Medicine 'for their discoveries concerning the molecular structure of nucleic acids and its significance for information transfer in living material.'

1963

23 January – Double Agent Kim Philby disappears having defected to the Soviet Union.

15 March – Ridge v. Baldwin, a landmark case in the law of judicial review, is decided on appeal: a public official is held to be wrongfully dismissed because he had no notice of the grounds on which the decision was made and no opportunity to be heard in his own defence.

27 March – Chairman of British Railways Dr Richard Beeching issues a report calling for huge cuts to the UK's rail network. This is expected to result in the closure of more than 2,000 railway stations as well as the scrapping of some 8,000 coaches and the loss of up to 68,000 jobs.

5 June – Profumo Affair: John Profumo, Secretary of State for War, admits to misleading Parliament and resigns over his affair with Christine Keeler.

1 July – Kim Philby named as the 'Third Man' in the Burgess and Maclean spy ring.

12 July – Pauline Reade, 16, is reported missing on her way to a dance in Gorton, Manchester, the first victim of the Moors murderers.

5 August – The United States, United Kingdom and Soviet Union sign a nuclear test ban treaty.

8 August – The Great Train Robbery takes place in Buckinghamshire.

5 September – Christine Keeler is arrested for perjury. On 6 December she is sentenced to nine months in prison.

17 September – RAF Fylingdales radar station on the North York Moors begins operation as part of the United States Ballistic Missile Early Warning System.

22 November – the assassination of American President John F. Kennedy, news of which reaches the UK just after 18:30 UTC.

1964

20 January – Eleven men go on trial at Buckinghamshire Assizes in Aylesbury charged in connection with the Great Train Robbery five months ago.

21 January – Government figures show that the average weekly wage is £16.

21 February – £10 banknotes are issued for the first time since the Second World War.

26 March – Verdicts are passed on ten men for their role in the Great Train Robbery after one of the longest criminal trials and longest jury retirals in English legal history.

30 March – Violent disturbances between Mods and Rockers at Clacton beach.

16 April – Sentence is passed on eleven men for their role in the Great Train Robbery, seven receiving 30 years each.

28 July – Winston Churchill retires from the House of Commons at the age of 89.

4 August – the first portable televisions go on sale.

13 August – Peter Anthony Allen, at Walton Prison in Liverpool, and Gwynne Owen Evans, at Strangeways Prison in Manchester, are hanged for the murder of John Alan Weston 7 April, the last executions to take place in the British Isles.

21 December – MPs vote 355 to 170 for the abolition of the death penalty, with the abolition likely to be confirmed before the end of next year. The death penalty has gradually fallen out of use over the last twenty years, with the two most recent executions having taken place in August this year. Some 90% of British households now own a television, compared to around 25% in 1953 and 65% in 1959.

1965

7 January – Identical twin brothers Ronnie and Reggie Kray, 31, are arrested on suspicion of running a protection racket in London.

8 July – Great Train Robber Ronald Biggs escapes from Wandsworth Prison.

24 July – Freddie Mills, former British boxing champion, is found shot in his car in Soho.

6 October – Ian Brady, a 27-year-old stock clerk from Hyde in Cheshire, is arrested for allegedly hacking 17-year-old apprentice electrician Edward Evans to death at a house on the Hattersley housing estate.

8 October – The Post Office Tower opens in London.

16 October – Police find a girl's body on Saddleworth Moor near Oldham in Lancashire. The body is quickly identified as that of Lesley Ann Downey.

29 October – Ian Brady and Myra Hindley appear in court, charged with the murders of Edward Evans (17), Lesley Ann Downey (10) and John Kilbride (12). The Race Relations Act outlaws public racial discrimination.

Charge Sheet Information

Roger Cordrey's Charge Sheet Information

Roger John Cordrey
No Fixed Abode.
42 years (30/5/21)
Florist
Male
White
5'9"
CRO 3716/42

Charges

Conspiracy to Rob
On divers day unknown between the first day of May 1963 and the ninth day of August 1963 in the County of Buckinghamshire conspired together and with other persons unknown to stop a mail with intent to rob the said mail.

Against the Peace of our Sovereign Lady the Queen, Her Crown and Dignity

Robbery
On the eighth day of August 1963, in the county of Buckinghamshire, being armed with offensive weapons or being together with other persons robbed Frank Dewhurst of 120 mailbags.

Contrary to Section 23(1) of the Larceny Act 1916

Receiving stolen goods
On a day unknown between the 7th and 15th days of August 1963 received £56,037 in money, the property of the Postmaster General knowing the same to have been stolen from and out of a mailbag and to have been sent by post.

Contrary to Section 54 Post Office Act 1953.

Receiving stolen goods
On a day unknown between the 7th and 15th days of August 1963 received £79,120 in money, the property of the Postmaster General knowing the same to have been stolen from and out of a mailbag and to have been sent by post.

Contrary to Section 54 Post Office Act 1953.

Receiving stolen goods
On a day unknown between the 7th and 15th days of August 1963 received £5,060 in money, the property of the Postmaster General knowing the same to have been stolen from and out of a mailbag and to have been sent by post.

Contrary to Section 54 Post Office Act 1953.

Previous convictions

16/12/41	Surrey Sessions	Embezzlement	Borstal training
		Embezzlement	
		Falsification of accounts	
		Falsification of accounts	
		Falsification of accounts	
		Falsification of accounts	
		Falsification of accounts	
		Falsification of accounts	
		Larceny as a servant	

Bill Boal's Charge Sheet Information

William Gerald Boal
22, Burnsthwaite Road,
Fulham,
London.
49 years (22/10/13) Durham
Precision Engineer
Male
White
6'00"
CRO Not known

Charges

Conspiracy to Rob

On divers day unknown between the first day of May 1963 and the ninth day of August 1963 in the County of Buckinghamshire conspired together and with other persons unknown to stop a mail with intent to rob the said mail.

Against the Peace of our Sovereign Lady the Queen, Her Crown and Dignity.

Robbery

On the eighth day of August 1963, in the county of Buckinghamshire, being armed with offensive weapons or being together with other persons robbed Frank Dewhurst of 120 mailbags.

Contrary to Section 23(1) of the Larceny Act 1916.

Receiving stolen goods

On a day unknown between the 7th and 15th days of August 1963 received £56,037 in money, the property of the Postmaster General knowing the same to have been stolen from and out of a mailbag and to have been sent by post.

Contrary to Section 54 Post Office Act 1953.

Receiving stolen goods

On a day unknown between the 7th and 15th days of August 1963 received £79,120 in money, the property of the Postmaster General knowing the same to have been stolen from and out of a mailbag and to have been sent by post.

Contrary to Section 54 Post Office Act 1953.

Receiving stolen goods

On a day unknown between the 7th and 15th days of August 1963 received £5,060 in money, the property of the Postmaster General knowing the same to have been stolen from and out of a mailbag and to have been sent by post.

Contrary to Section 54 Post Office Act 1953.

Previous convictions

2/9/47	Feltham Magistrates Crt	Found on enclosed premises for an unlawful purpose	Fined £20
24/1/49	Surrey Quarter Sessions	Receiving stolen property Receiving stolen property Fraudulently extracting electricity	18 months imprisonment
18/4/63	Mortlake Magistrates Crt	Assault on Police	Fined £10
			Bound over 1 year

Charlie Wilson's Charge Sheet Information

Charles Frederick Wilson
45, Crescent Lane,
Clapham,
London, SW4
31 years (30/6/32) Battersea
Greengrocer
Male
White
6'00"
CRO 5010/54

Charges

Conspiracy to Rob
On divers day unknown between the first day of May 1963 and the ninth day of August 1963 in the County of Buckinghamshire conspired together and with other persons unknown to stop a mail with intent to rob the said mail.

Against the Peace of our Sovereign Lady the Queen, Her Crown and Dignity

Robbery
On the eighth day of August 1963, in the county of Buckinghamshire, being armed with offensive weapons or being

together with other persons robbed Frank Dewhurst of 120 mailbags.

Contrary to Section 23(1) of the Larceny Act 1916.

Previous convictions

20/1/54	South Western Magistrates Court	Theft of petrol	Fined £5
20/12/56	South Western Magistrates Court	Suspected person loitering with intent to steal from motor vehicles	Conditional Discharge 12 months
16/1/58	County of London Sessions	Receiving stolen property Receiving stolen property	12 months imprisonment
26/5/59	Central Criminal Court	Conspiracy to steal	30 months imprisonment

Gordon Goody's Charge Sheet Information

Douglas Gordon Goody
6, Commondale,
Putney,
London.
SW15.
33 years (11/3/30) Putney, London.
Hairdresser
Male
White
5'11"
CRO 4290/46

Charges

Conspiracy to Rob
On divers day unknown between the first day of May 1963 and the ninth day of August 1963 in the County of Buckinghamshire conspired together and with other persons unknown to stop a mail with intent to rob the said mail.

Against the Peace of our Sovereign Lady the Queen, Her Crown and Dignity.

Robbery

On the eighth day of August 1963, in the county of Buckinghamshire, being armed with offensive weapons or being together with other persons robbed Frank Dewhurst of 120 mailbags.

Contrary to Section 23(1) of the Larceny Act 1916.

Previous Convictions

22/6/45	Lambeth Juvenile Court	Stealing two lamps	Bound over 1 year
		Stealing a pedal cycle	
18/1/46	Lambeth Juvenile Court	Receiving stolen jersey	Bound over 1 year
21/1/48	County of London Sessions	Shopbreaking and stealing coat valued at 18 guineas	Bound over 2 years.
		Stealing cigarettes and clothing valued at £15	Bound over 2 years.
		Throwing stone at plate glass window	Fined £10
2/3/48	Central Criminal Court	Robbery with Violence	21 months imprisonment and 2 strokes of the birch
20/10/49	Bow Street Magistrates Court	Suspected person loitering with intent to steal from motor cars.	3 months imprisonment
8/11/49	County of London Sessions	Shopbreaking and larceny	9 months imprisonment
18/5/55	Surrey Quarter Sessions	Housebreaking with intent	Conditional discharge 1 year
15/3/56	Surrey Quarter Sessions	Shopbreaking and stealing jewellery	3 years imprisonment on each concurrent
		Taking and driving away a motor car	Disqualified for 7 years.

20/2/61	Richmond Magistrates Court	Possessing a firearm whilst a prohibited person	Fined £8 and ordered to pay 3 guineas costs
		Possessing ammunition while a prohibited person	Weapon and ammunition confiscated

Ronnie Biggs' Charge Sheet Information

Ronald Arthur Biggs
37, Alpine Road,
Redhill,
Surrey.
34 years (born 8/8/29) Lambeth, London.
Carpenter and builder
Male
White
6'00"
CRO Not known

Charges

Conspiracy to Rob
On divers day unknown between the first day of May 1963 and the ninth day of August 1963 in the County of Buckinghamshire conspired together and with other persons unknown to stop a mail with intent to rob the said mail.

Against the Peace of our Sovereign Lady the Queen, Her Crown and Dignity.

Robbery
On the eighth day of August 1963, in the county of Buckinghamshire, being armed with offensive weapons or being together with other persons robbed Frank Dewhurst of 120 mailbags.

Contrary to Section 23(1) of the Larceny Act 1916.

Previous Convictions

9/2/45	Lambeth Juvenile Court	Stealing pencils from a shop	Dismissed
8/6/45	Lambeth Juvenile Court	Stealing radio parts from a church store	Bound over 12 months and 10 shillings surety
16/11/45	Lambeth Juvenile Court	Stealing a watch	Bound over 12 months and £1 surety
17/2/49	County of London Sessions	Shopbreaking and larceny	6 months imprisonment
		Housebreaking and larceny	
		False representation of national registration card	
28/7/49	North London Magistrates Court	Taking and Driving Away motor car	2 months imprisonment
		Use of motor car	Fined 40 shillings
		No certificate of insurance	Disqualified from driving 12 months
		Misuse of motor fuel	
30/11/49	Essex Quarter Sessions	Shopbreaking and larceny	Borstal Training (Escaped 4/2/50, but re-captured)
28/3/50	Central Criminal Court	Robbery (6 cases taken into consideration)	3 years imprisonment
24/3/53	County of London Sessions	Garage breaking and stealing motor car (1 case taken into consideration)	3 years imprisonment
30/3/53	Buckinghamshire Quarter Sessions	Burglary and stealing property valued at 18 shillings	4 years imprisonment concurrent with sentence of 24/3/53
		Housebreaking and stealing property value of £5, £164. 15s and £22. 12s (3 cases taken into consideration)	

15/6/56	Surrey Appeals Committee	Stealing paint from a building site	Probation Order 2 years
		Stealing a pedal cycle	
2/4/58	Dorset Quarter Sessions	Taking a motor vehicle without consent	12 months imprisonment
		Receiving stolen toilet goods	
		Receiving stolen car rug	
25/4/58	Surrey Appeals Committee	Stealing paint Stealing cycle (offences of 15/6/56)	18 months imprisonment on each concurrent with 2/4/58

Jim Hussey's Charge Sheet Information

James Hussey
8, Edridge House,
Dog Kennel Hill,
East Dulwich,
London, SE22.
31 years (8/4/33) Camberwell
Painter and decorator
Male
White
5'11"
CRO 40455/49

Charges

Conspiracy to Rob
On divers day unknown between the first day of May 1963 and the ninth day of August 1963 in the County of Buckinghamshire conspired together and with other persons unknown to stop a mail with intent to rob the said mail.

Against the Peace of our Sovereign Lady the Queen, Her Crown and Dignity.

Robbery

On the eighth day of August 1963, in the county of Buckinghamshire, being armed with offensive weapons or being together with other persons robbed Frank Dewhurst of 120 mailbags.

Contrary to Section 23(1) of the Larceny Act 1916.

Previous convictions

23/8/46	Lambeth Juvenile Court	Stealing sports equipment from a school	Dismissed
		Stealing sports equipment from a school	Dismissed
		Stealing sports equipment from a school	Dismissed
18/11/49	Lambeth Juvenile Court	Unauthorised taking of a motor vehicle	Fined £4
		No insurance	Disqualified 12 months
16/5/50	Central Criminal Court	Grievous Bodily Harm with Intent	18 months imprisonment
		Assault occasioning Actual Bodily Harm	
13/6/52	Lambeth Magistrates Court	Grievous Bodily Harm Grievous Bodily Harm	Fined £12
5/9/53	Bow Street Magistrates Court	Suspected person loitering with intent to steal from motor vehicles.	Probation Order 1 year
25/6/56	Lambeth Magistrates Court	Tampering with a motor vehicle	Fined £5
17/12/58	Manchester Crown Court	Warehousebreaking and larceny of cigarettes and tobacco valued together at £10,820.1s.10d	3 years imprisonment

		Grievous Bodily Harm with intent to resist arrest	2 years imprisonment
		Grievous Bodily Harm with intent to resist arrest	2 years imprisonment
18/12/62	Munich, Germany	Pickpocketing	5 months imprisonment Deported to the UK

Leonard Field's Charge Sheet Information

Leonard Dennis Field
262, Green Lane,
London. N16.
31 years (--/--/31) Not known
Merchant Navy seaman
Male
White
5'10"
CRO No Trace

Charges

Conspiracy to Rob
On divers day unknown between the first day of May 1963 and the ninth day of August 1963 in the County of Buckinghamshire conspired together and with other persons unknown to stop a mail with intent to rob the said mail.

Against the Peace of our Sovereign Lady the Queen, Her Crown and Dignity.

Robbery
On the eighth day of August 1963, in the county of Buckinghamshire, being armed with offensive weapons or being together with other persons robbed Frank Dewhurst of 120 mailbags.

Contrary to Section 23(1) of the Larceny Act 1916.

Previous convictions

17/5/51	Clerkenwell Magistrates Court	Suspected person loitering with intent to steal from motor vehicles	Fined 40 shillings

Brian Field's Charge Sheet Information

Brian Arthur Field
Kabri,
Pangbourne,
Berkshire.
29 years (15/12/34)
Solicitor's managing clerk
Male
White
6'00"
CRO No Trace (no previous convictions)

Charges

Conspiracy to Rob
On divers day unknown between the first day of May 1963 and the ninth day of August 1963 in the County of Buckinghamshire conspired together and with other persons unknown to stop a mail with intent to rob the said mail.

Against the Peace of our Sovereign Lady the Queen, Her Crown and Dignity.

Robbery
On the eighth day of August 1963, in the county of Buckinghamshire, being armed with offensive weapons or being together with other persons robbed Frank Dewhurst of 120 mailbags.

Contrary to Section 23(1) of the Larceny Act 1916.

Receiving Stolen Goods
On a day unknown between seventh and seventeenth days of August 1963, received £100,900 in money the property of the

Postmaster General knowing the same to have been stolen from and out of a mailbag and to have been sent by post.

Contrary to Section 54 of the Post Office Act 1953.

Previous convictions

None

John Wheater's Charge Sheet Information

John Denby Wheater
Otteways Lane,
Ashtead,
Surrey.
41 years (17/12/21) Not known
Solicitor
Male
White
6'00"
CRO No Trace (no previous convictions)

Charges

Conspiracy to Rob
On divers day unknown between the first day of May 1963 and the ninth day of August 1963 in the County of Buckinghamshire conspired together and with other persons unknown to stop a mail with intent to rob the said mail.

Against the Peace of our Sovereign Lady the Queen, Her Crown and Dignity.

Between the seventh day of August 1963 and the tenth day of September 1963 in the County of London well knowing that one Leonard Dennis Field had robbed Frank Dewhurst od 120 mailbags did comfort, harbour and assist and maintain the said Leonard Dennis Field.

Against the Peace of our Sovereign Lady the Queen, Her Crown and Dignity.

Previous convictions

None

Roy James' Charge Sheet Information

Roy John James
14, Ryder's Terrace,
St John's Wood,
NW8.
28 years (30/8/35) Not known
Silversmith
Male
White
5'8"
CRO 17638/56

Charges

Conspiracy to Rob
On divers day unknown between the first day of May 1963 and the ninth day of August 1963 in the County of Buckinghamshire conspired together and with other persons unknown to stop a mail with intent to rob the said mail.

Against the Peace of our Sovereign Lady the Queen, Her Crown and Dignity.

Robbery
On the eighth day of August 1963, in the county of Buckinghamshire, being armed with offensive weapons or being together with other persons robbed Frank Dewhurst of 120 mailbags.

Contrary to Section 23(1) of the Larceny Act 1916.

Previous Convictions

3/5/56	West London Magistrates Court	Stealing a vacuum cleaner valued at £10	Probation Order 1 year on each concurrent
		Stealing cine projector valued at £87.10s	
2/7/56	Police Court, Jersey, CI	Larceny from motor cars	3 days Hard labour
		Stealing sunglasses valued at 16s	
18/10/56	Middlesex Quarter Sessions	Receiving stolen motor car tools valued at £12	3 months imprisonment
27/2/57	West London Magistrates Court	Taking and driving away without consent	Fined £5
		No Insurance	Fined £1
		Stealing a car wheel and car radio valued together at £30.12s.6d	Fined £5
11/7/58	County of London Sessions	Shopbreaking and larceny valued at £478	3 years imprisonment in corrective training on each concurrent
		Shopbreaking and larceny valued at £188. 9s	
13/6/63	County of London Sessions	Dangerous Driving	Fined £15 with £15 costs

Bob Welch's Charge Sheet Information

Robert Alfred Welch
No Fixed Abode
35 years (12/3/29)
Club proprietor and bookmaker
Male
White
5'10"
CRO 61730/58

Charges

Conspiracy to Rob
On divers day unknown between the first day of May 1963 and the ninth day of August 1963 in the County of Buckinghamshire conspired together and with other persons unknown to stop a mail with intent to rob the said mail.

Against the peace of our Sovereign Lady the Queen, Her Crown and Dignity.

Robbery
On the eighth day of August 1963, in the county of Buckinghamshire, being armed with offensive weapons or being together with other persons robbed Frank Dewhurst of 120 mailbags.

Contrary to Section 23(1) of the Larceny Act 1916.

Previous convictions

1/10/58	County of London Sessions	Receiving stolen coffee, tea and custard powder valued together at £2,616. 13s.2d	9 months imprisonment
21/3/63	Bow Street Magistrates Court	Selling intoxicating liquor without a licence	Fined £210
		Selling intoxicating liquor without a licence	
		Selling intoxicating liquor without a licence	
		Selling intoxicating liquor without a licence	

John Daly's Charge Sheet Information

John Thomas Daly
63A, Eaton Square,
London, SW1.
32 years (6/6/31) New Ross, Eire.
Antique Dealer
Male
White
5'11"
CRO 33521/48

Charges

Conspiracy to Rob
On divers day unknown between the first day of May 1963 and the ninth day of August 1963 in the County of Buckinghamshire conspired together and with other persons unknown to stop a mail with intent to rob the said mail.

Against the peace of our Sovereign Lady the Queen, Her Crown and Dignity.

Robbery
On the eighth day of August 1963, in the county of Buckinghamshire, being armed with offensive weapons or being together with other persons robbed Frank Dewhurst of 120 mailbags.

Contrary to Section 23(1) of the Larceny Act 1916.

Previous Convictions

7/8/48	Woking Petty Sessions	Stealing £1 from a shop	Bound Over
23/12/48	West London Mags Court	Unauthorised taking of motor car	Police Detention 1 day
26/1/50	County of London Sessions	Burglary and larceny / Burglary and larceny	Borstal training

15/10/52	County of Middlesex Sessions	Shopbreaking and larceny Burglary	Imprisoned 15 months
		Unauthorised taking of a motor car	Disqualified 3 years
19/11/53	South Western Mags Ct	Suspected person loitering with intent to steal from motor cars.	Fined £10 or 6 weeks imprisonment (Committed 25/2/54)
13/1/54	Bow Street Mags Court	Suspected person loitering with intent to steal from motor cars	3 months imprisonment on each concurrent
		Assault Police	
31/12/54	Kingston Borough Mags Court	Stealing 3 pairs of trousers valued at £11, from a shop display stand	6 months imprisonment
29/3/60	Northampton Borough Quarter Sessions	Attempted shopbreaking	1 year imprisonment
		Estreating bail	£50 estreated

Jimmy White's Charge Sheet Information

James White
Flat 4 Claverley Mansions,
Littlestone,
Kent.
43 years (21/2/20)
Café owner
Male
White
5'7"
CRO 26113/55

Charges

Conspiracy to Rob
On divers day unknown between the first day of May 1963 and the ninth day of August 1963 in the County of Buckinghamshire conspired together and with other persons unknown to stop a mail with intent to rob the said mail.

Against the peace of our Sovereign Lady the Queen, Her Crown and Dignity.

Robbery
On the eighth day of August 1963, in the county of Buckinghamshire, being armed with offensive weapons or being together with other persons robbed Frank Dewhurst of 120 mailbags.

Contrary to Section 23(1) of the Larceny Act 1916.

Previous convictions

7/7/55	Hendon Magistrates Court	Receiving cigarettes and tobacco valued at £900	Probation 3 years
14/5/58	Acton Magistrates Court	Receiving jewellery valued at £40	6 months imprisonment
		Stealing by finding a wallet valued at £2.10s	3 months imprisonment consecutive
23/6/58	Bedfordshire Quarter Sessions	Shopbreaking and stealing photographic equipment valued at £377. 9s.3d	18 months imprisonment to run consecutively from sentence of 14/5/58

Buster Edwards' Charge Sheet Information

Ronald Christopher Edwards
No fixed abode.
32 years (27th January 1931) Lambeth
Club owner
Male

White
5'6"
CRO 33535/61

Charges

Conspiracy to Rob
On divers day unknown between the first day of May 1963 and the ninth day of August 1963 in the County of Buckinghamshire conspired together and with other persons unknown to stop a mail with intent to rob the said mail.

Against the peace of our Sovereign Lady the Queen, Her Crown and Dignity.

Robbery
On the eighth day of August 1963, in the county of Buckinghamshire, being armed with offensive weapons or being together with other persons robbed Frank Dewhurst of 120 mailbags.

Contrary to Section 23(1) of the Larceny Act 1916.

Previous convictions

18/7/50	RAF Court Martial,	Breaking and Entering	42 days imprisonment
	Newark	Stealing cigarettes Wilful damage	
3/11/60	Lambeth Magistrates Ct	Selling intoxicating Liquor without a Licence	Fined £50
4/1/61	Old Street Magistrates Ct	No Insurance	Fined £10 Disqualified
11/5/61	West London Magistrates	Attempted larceny from van	Fined £15
	Ct	Assault on Police	Fined £20
21/11/61	County of London Session	Driving whilst Disqualified	Imprisoned 14 days Disqualified 2 years

Bruce Reynolds' Charge Sheet information

Bruce Reynolds
Villa Cap Martin,
Braddons Hill Road East,
Torquay,
Cornwall.
31 years (7/9/31) Strand, London.
Antiques dealer and car dealer
Male
White
6'1"
CRO 41212/48

Charges

Conspiracy to Rob
On divers day unknown between the first day of May 1963 and the ninth day of August 1963 in the County of Buckinghamshire conspired together and with other persons unknown to stop a mail with intent to rob the said mail.

Against the peace of our Sovereign Lady the Queen, Her Crown and Dignity.

Robbery
On the eighth day of August 1963, in the county of Buckinghamshire, being armed with offensive weapons or being together with other persons robbed Frank Dewhurst of 120 mailbags.

Contrary to Section 23(1) of the Larceny Act 1916.

Previous convictions

17/9/48	South Western Police Court	Assault on police	Fined 20 shillings
		Riding a cycle without lights	Fined 30 shillings
20/4/49	South Western Magistrates Court	Larceny of cigarettes and money valued together at £70.3s.2d	Bound over 1 year

Date	Court	Charge	Sentence
1/6/49	County of London Sessions	Shopbreaking and larceny.	Borstal Training
21/3/50	County of London Sessions	Housebreaking and larceny	Borstal training on each concurrent
		Workshop breaking and larceny	
		Shopbreaking and larceny	
		Factorybreaking with intent	
25/10/50	County of London Sessions	Shopbreaking and larceny	18 months imprisonment
		Shopbreaking and larceny	
		Officebreaking with intent	Borstal training
		Larceny	
		Larceny	
29/10/52	South Western Magistrates Court	No Insurance	Fined £10
18/11/52	County of London Sessions	Shopbreaking and larceny of five wirelesses valued together at £89	3 years imprisonment
		Shopbreaking and larceny of two overcoats valued together at £97	3 years imprisonment
		Unauthorised taking of motor vehicle	9 months imprisonment All concurrent
26/1/55	Lambeth Magistrates Court	Larceny of portable wireless set valued at £18 from shop display	6 months imprisonment
17/5/56	South Western Magistrates Court	Receiving a stolen heat lamp	Fined £25 or 3 months
16/1/58	Central Criminal Court	Malicious wounding with intent	30 months imprisonment
		Assault on Police	6 months imprisonment
		Assault on Police	6 months imprisonment All consecutive
30/5/63	Ongar Magistrates Court	Poaching	Fined £10

Court Result Sheets

Defendant	Roger Cordrey
Date of arrest	14/8/63
Bail or custody	Custody
Dates of trial	20/1/64 to 16/4/64
Name of Court	Aylesbury Crown Court
Solicitors	Hardcastle, Sanders & Armitage
Counsel 1	J.G. Leach
Counsel 2	I.T.R. Davidson
Counsel 3	None

Conspiracy to Rob
Plea: Guilty   Verdict: Guilty

Robbery
Plea: Not Guilty   Verdict: Jury Discharged

Receiving stolen goods x 3
Plea: Guilty   Verdict: Guilty

Sentence	1. 20 years imprisonment 3, 4, 5, 20 years imprisonment. To run concurrently.
Released	1971

Defendant	Bill Boal
Date of arrest	14/8/63
Bail or custody	Custody
Dates of trial	20/1/64 to 16/4/64
Name of Court	Aylesbury Crown Court
Solicitors	Malcolm Davis & Co
Counsel 1	W.A. Sime QC
Counsel 2	E. Eyre
Counsel 3	None

Conspiracy to Rob

Plea: Not Guilty   Verdict: Guilty

Robbery

Plea: Not Guilty   Verdict: Guilty

Receiving stolen goods x 3

Plea: Not Guilty	Verdict: Jury Discharged
Sentence	1. 21 years imprisonment 2. 24 years imprisonment. To run concurrently
Released	Died in prison in 1970

Defendant	Charlie Wilson
Date of arrest	23/8/63
Bail or custody	Custody
Dates of trial	20/1/64 to 16/4/64
Name of Court	Aylesbury Crown Court
Solicitors	Sampson & Co
Counsel 1	J.C. Mathew
Counsel 2	J.N. Speed
Counsel 3	W.M. Howard

Conspiracy to Rob

Plea: Not Guilty   Verdict: Guilty

Robbery

Plea: Not Guilty	Verdict: Guilty
Sentence	1. 25 years imprisonment 2. 30 years imprisonment. To run concurrently.
Released	1978

Defendant	Gordon Goody
Date of arrest	3/10/63
Bail or custody	Custody
Dates of trial	20/1/64 to 16/4/64
Name of Court	Aylesbury Crown Court
Solicitors	Lesser & Co
Counsel 1	Sebag Shaw QC
Counsel 2	Wilfred Fordham
Counsel 3	C. Salmon

Conspiracy to Rob
Plea: Not Guilty   Verdict: Guilty

Robbery
Plea: Not Guilty   Verdict: Guilty
Sentence   1. 25 years imprisonment 2. 30 years
                        imprisonment. To run concurrently
Released   1975

Defendant	Ronnie Biggs
Date of arrest	4/9/63
Bail or custody	Custody
Dates of trial	20/1/64 to 16/4/64
Name of Court	Aylesbury Crown Court
Solicitors	Lesser & Co
Counsel 1	Wilfred Fordham
Counsel 2	C. Salmon

Conspiracy to Rob
Plea: Not Guilty   Verdict: Guilty

Robbery
Plea: Not Guilty   Verdict: Guilty
Sentence   1. 25 years imprisonment 2. 30 years
                        imprisonment. To run concurrently.
Released   2009

Defendant	Tommy Wisbey
Date of arrest	11/9/63
Bail or custody	Custody
Dates of trial	20/1/64 to 16/4/64
Name of Court	Aylesbury Crown Court
Solicitors	Lincoln & Lincoln
Counsel 1	J.A. Grieves QC
Counsel 2	Hon P.M. Packenham
Counsel 3	None

Conspiracy to Rob

Plea: Not Guilty	Verdict: Guilty

Robbery

Plea: Not Guilty	Verdict: Guilty
Sentence	1. 25 years imprisonment 2. 30 years imprisonment. To run concurrently.
Released	1976

Defendant	Jim Hussey
Date of arrest	7/9/63
Bail or custody	Custody
Dates of trial	20/1/64 to 16/4/64
Name of Court	Aylesbury Crown Court
Solicitors	Lincoln & Lincoln
Counsel 1	R.K. Brown QC
Counsel 2	R.G. Freeman
Counsel 3	None

Conspiracy to Rob

Plea: Not Guilty	Verdict: Guilty

Robbery

Plea: Not Guilty	Verdict: Guilty
Sentence	1. 25 years imprisonment 2. 30 years imprisonment. To run concurrently.
Released	1975

Defendant	Lennie Field
Date of arrest	14/9/63
Bail or custody	Custody
Dates of trial	20/1/64 to 16/4/64
Name of Court	Aylesbury Crown Court
Solicitors	Lessor & Co
Counsel 1	Michael V. Argyle QC
Counsel 2	E.F. Jowitt
Counsel 3	None

Conspiracy to Rob
Plea: Not Guilty   Verdict: Guilty

Robbery
Plea: Not Guilty   Verdict: Jury Discharged

Conspiracy to Obstruct Justice
Plea: Not Guilty   Verdict: Guilty

Sentence	1. 25 years imprisonment 3. 5 years imprisonment. To run concurrently.
Released	1967

Defendant	Brian Field
Date of arrest	15/9/63
Bail or custody	Custody
Dates of trial	20/1/64 to 16/4/64
Name of Court	Aylesbury Crown Court
Solicitors	Lipson, Romney & Co
Counsel 1	C. Lewis Hawser QC
Counsel 2	I.S. Richard
Counsel 3	G.C. Heseltine

Conspiracy to Rob
Plea: Not Guilty   Verdict: Guilty

Robbery
Plea: Not Guilty   Verdict: Not Guilty

Receiving stolen goods
Plea: Not Guilty   Verdict: Not Guilty

Conspiracy to Obstruct Justice
Plea: Not Guilty   Verdict: Guilty

Sentence	1. 25 years imprisonment 4. 5 years imprisonment. To run concurrently.
Released	1967

Defendant	John Wheater
Date of arrest	17/10/63
Bail or custody	Bail
Dates of trial	20/1/64 to 16/4/64
Name of Court	Aylesbury Crown Court
Solicitors	John Wheater
Counsel 1	G.R. Swanwick QC
Counsel 2	A.F. Waley
Counsel 3	None

Conspiracy to Rob
Plea: Not Guilty   Verdict: Not Guilty

Conspiracy to Obstruct Justice

Plea: Not Guilty	Verdict: Guilty
Sentence	2. 3 years imprisonment.
Released	1966

Defendant	Roy James
Date of arrest	10/12/63
Bail or custody	Custody
Dates of trial	20/1/64 to 16/4/64
Name of Court	Aylesbury Crown Court
Solicitors	Samson & Co
Counsel 1	W.M. Howard
Counsel 2	J.N. Speed
Counsel 3	J.C. Mathew

Conspiracy to Rob
Plea: Not Guilty   Verdict: Guilty

Robbery
Plea: Not Guilty   Verdict: Guilty

Receiving stolen goods x 2

Plea: Not Guilty	Verdict: Jury Discharged
Sentence	1. 25 years imprisonment 2. 30 years imprisonment. To run concurrently.
Released	1975

Defendant	Bob Welch
Date of arrest	25/10/63
Bail or custody	Custody
Dates of trial	20/1/64 to 16/4/64
Name of Court	Aylesbury Crown Court
Solicitors	Lincoln & Lincoln
Counsel 1	F. Ashe Lincoln QC
Counsel 2	J.L. Gamgee
Counsel 3	None

Conspiracy to Rob

Plea: Not Guilty	Verdict: Guilty

Robbery

Plea: Not Guilty	Verdict: Guilty
Sentence	1. 25 years imprisonment 2. 30 years imprisonment. To run concurrently.
Released	1976

Defendant	John Daly
Date of arrest	3/12/63
Bail or custody	Custody
Dates of trial	20/1/64 to 16/4/64
Name of Court	Aylesbury Crown Court
Solicitors	Lessor & Co
Counsel 1	W.A.L. Raeburn
Counsel 2	Wilfred Fordham
Counsel 3	J.N. Speed

Conspiracy to Rob

Plea: Not Guilty	Verdict: Not Guilty

Robbery

Plea: Not Guilty	Verdict: Not Guilty
Sentence	Acquitted on all charges.
Released	Acquitted on all charges.

Defendant	Jimmy White
Date of arrest	21/4/65
Bail or custody	Custody
Dates of trial	
Name of Court	
Solicitors	Lesser & Co
Counsel 1	Not known
Counsel 2	Not Known
Counsel 3	Not Known

Conspiracy to Rob
Plea: Not Guilty   Verdict: Guilty

Robbery
Plea: Not Guilty   Verdict: Guilty

Sentence	1. 25 years imprisonment 2. 30 years imprisonment. To run concurrently.
Released	1975

Defendant	Buster Edwards
Date of arrest	19/9/65
Bail or custody	Custody
Dates of trial	8 to 9 December 1966
Name of Court	Nottingham Assizes
Solicitors	Lesser & Co
Counsel 1	Not known
Counsel 2	Not known
Counsel 3	Not known

Conspiracy to Rob
Plea: Not Guilty   Verdict: Guilty

Robbery
Plea: Not Guilty   Verdict: Guilty

Sentence	1. 15 years imprisonment 2. 12 years imprisonment. To run concurrently.
Released	1975

Defendant	Bruce Reynolds
Date of arrest	8/11/68
Bail or custody	Custody
Dates of trial	14/1/69
Name of Court	Aylesbury Crown Court
Solicitors	Lesser & Co
Counsel 1	Not known
Counsel 2	Not known
Counsel 2	Not known

Conspiracy to Rob

Plea: Not Guilty   Verdict: Guilty

Robbery

Plea: Not Guilty   Verdict: Guilty

Sentence   1. 25 years imprisonment 2. 25 years imprisonment
To run concurrently.

Released   1978

Metropolitan Police Central Records of Service

Thomas Marius Joseph BUTLER M.B.E.
Born 21/7/12 Shepherds Bush 5'9¼"
Joined 22/10/34 Warrant Number 74/123749
Elementary Education and then Warehouseman
Single

Date	District	Borough	Promoted to:
22/10/34	TS	Training School	PC
4/3/35	F	Hammersmith	
30/5/38	C	Westminster	DC
1/9/41	C1	Murder Squad	
15/7/46	G	Hackney	DS(2)
15/8/49	N	Islington	DS(1)
3/10/49	D	Paddington	
2/8/55	C8	Flying Squad	DI
30/6/58	B.P.U. Cyprus	B.P.U. Cyprus	DCI
25/11/58	Re-join M.P.	Re-join Met	
2/11/59	C8	Flying Squad	DSupt
8/7/63	1 HQ	S.W. London HQ	DCS
1/10/63	C8	Flying Squad	
21/7/67	Service extended	Age 55 years.	Service extended
31/12/68 Discharged*	Discharged	34 years 2 m 10 days	Exemplary
20/4/70	Died	Died	

* Having been granted special authority to extend his service, he did not have to resign, but left when the extension ended.

CENTRAL RECORD OF SERVICE

Rank: *Chief Det. Supt. 4* / *Supt 1st Class C.I.D.* — 3rd Class

Name: Thomas Marius Joseph Surname: BUTLER "MBE."

Warrant No. 1234 LS A-5 (Records) No. 30. SHORT L

Former Warrant No.

		HEIGHT		PREVIOUS HISTORY		Police or Other Public Service. Service in H.M. Forces and Period on Reserve	Decorations	Married or Single	No. of Children	TRANSFERS			
Date of Joining	Date of Birth	Place of Birth	Ft.	Ins.	Education	Occupation					Date	Div.	Date	Div.
22.10.1934	2.4.1912	Shepherds Bush London	5	9¾	Elementary	Warehouseman		M.B.E.	S		14.3.35	F		
Division to which Posted K								8 FEB 1957			30.5.38	C	31.1.02	
											1.9.41	C1		
											15.7/46	G		
											15.8.49	N		
											3.10.49	D		
											2.3.55	C.8		
											30.6.58			
											22.10.58	APW CYPRUS		

EXAMINATIONS

DURING PROBATIONARY PERIOD				EDUCATIONAL EXAMS. DURING SERVICE			TECHNICAL EXAMS			SPECIAL EXAMS		
	Police Duty	Education	First Aid	2nd Class Passed / Failed	1st Class Passed / Failed	Uniform	C.I.D.	Passed	Failed	Type	Passed	Failed
Training School	112	354	Q	Ex	6.39	Sergeant		16 DEC 1939		Motor Driving		
3 Months						Stn. Sergt.	1st Cl. Sergt.			Mounted Branch		
6 Months	Passed 3/5/35					Inspr.	2nd Cl. Inspr.			Pistol Shooting 17-5-55		
9 Months						S.D. or Dist Inspr.	1st Cl. Inspr.			PISTOLS May 1959		
12 Months	Passed No. 354/35 (Exam 62%)					Ch. Inspector	Ch. Inspector					

ADVANCEMENTS IN PAY

FIRST AID EXAMINATION					PROMOTIONS AND APPOINTMENTS				
Date	Result	Uniform	Date	C.I.D.	Date				
26.39 P		Actg. Sergt.		Constable	30.5.38				
1957 P		Sergeant		2nd Cl. Sergeant	15-7-46				
		Stn. or Clk. Sergt.		1st Cl. Sergeant	15.8.49				
		Inspector		2nd Class Inspector	1.7.54				
		S.D. or Dist. Insp		1st Class Inspector	1.4.55				
		Ch. Inspector		Superintendent	1.22.8.10.59				
		Superintendent		Ch. Constable	8.7.63				
		Ch. Constable							

SERVICE AT A NAVAL OR MILITARY STATION FROM WHICH THE OFFICER WAS WITHDRAWN ON GENERAL REDUCTION OF ESTABLISHMENT FOR REASONS OF ECONOMY

MILITARY STATION

Discharged on 31st December, 1968 Age

CERTIFICATE OF CONDUCT: EXEMPLARY

Pension H.O. Authority No. ... Date 24th December, 1968

AGE ON RETIREMENT 56 SERVICE 34 Years 2 months 10 days

DIED 20-4-70 AF35/70/237

No.	Date of P.O.	Amount	COMMENDATIONS AND AWARDS. By whom and for what Service	No.	Date of P.O.	REPORTS
1.	15.3.37		Comm. for sagacity			
2	31.12.37		Comm. Case of attempted larceny (M.O.O.)			Commendation (cont)
3	31.5.39		Comm. Case of demanding money with menaces (W.O.O.)	23	1.5.53	Comm. For valuable assistance in a case of murder.
4.	17.6.40		Comm. Case of shopbreaking	24	4.8.55	Comm. For ability & perseverance in a difficult case of abortion (W.O.O.)
5	6.3.41		Comm. Case of shopbreaking			
6	28.5.42		Comm. Case of receiving (W.O.O.)	25	10.2.56	Comm. For ability and determination in arresting a persistent and troublesome safe breaker. (W.O.O.)
7	10.9.42		Comm. Difficult case under Food Orders & Defence Regs. (W.O.O.)			
8	30.10.42		Comm. Case of larceny & receiving (W.O.O.)	26	29.3.56	Comm. For ability and perseverance in a case of robbery (W.O.O.)
9	11.5.43		Comm. Case of receiving (W.O.O.)			
10	10.9.43		Comm. Case of warehousebreaking (W.O.O.)	27	20.4.56	Comm. For ability and determination in arresting two frolic' criminals (W.O.O.)
11	28.1.44		Comm. For ability & perseverance in a case of forgery (W.A.O.)			
12	18.2.44		Comm. Difficult case of receiving W.O.O.	28	18.5.56	Comm. For ability and determination in arresting a persistent criminal (W.O.O.)
13	5.1.45		Case of conspiracy & larceny			
14	1.6.45		Comm. Case of house-breaking (W.O.O.)	29	5.6.56	Comm. For ability and persistence in a case of robbery with violence (W.O.O.)
15	28.8.46		Comm. Case of Receiving			
16	26.3.46		Comm. For skill in a case of larceny and conspiracy to receive (W.O.O.)	30	27.11.56	Comm. For ability in a case of grievous bodily harm. Also commend. at the C.C.C. (W.O.O.)
17	30.8.46		Comm. For zeal in a case of receiving			
18	12.9.47		Comm. For alertness in a case of warehouse breaking W.O.O.	31	9.4.57	Comm. For ability and persistence in a case of conspiracy to steal (W.O.O.)
19	5.10.48		Comm. For perseverance in a case of robbery (W.O.O.)			
20	31.1.50		Comm. For ability in a case of larceny mailbags. (W.O.O.)			
21	15.2.50		Comm. For ability in a case of false pretences			
22	24.7.51		Comm. For valuable assistance in a case of abortion (W.A.O.)			

CENTRAL RECORD OF SERVICE—CONTINUATION SHEET (No. *1*).

Rank *D/. Ch. Insp.*   Name *Thomas Marius Joseph*   Surname *BUTLER*   Warrant No. *123749*

Former Warrant No. ....

M.P.-34-2109/8x   w103

No.	Date of P.O.	Amount.	COMMENDATIONS AND AWARDS. (By whom and for what service)	No.	Date of P.O.	REPORTS
32.	10.6.58		Commr:- For valuable assistance in a complicated and difficult case of conspiracy to pervert the course of justice. Also commended at the C.C.C. by the D.P.P. (Woo) 020/57/505			
	31.67		Awarded The M.B.E. by Her Majesty The Queen.			

Francis Arthur WILLIAMS
Born 15/7/17 Ebbw Vale 5'10¼"
Joined 27/6/38 Warrant Number 09/126982
Elementary Education and then Joiner
Married with 4 children

Date	District	Borough	Promoted to:
27/6/38	TS	Training School	PC
September 1938?	N	Islington	
4/11/46	R	Greenwich	DC
7/1/52	M	Southwark	DS(2)
11/10/54	R	Greenwich	
26/11/56	L	Lambeth	DS(1)
4/1/60	C8	Flying Squad	
27/3/61	M	Southwark	DI
9/10/61	C8	Flying Squad	
3/2/64	M	Southwark	DCI
1/11/65	C8	Flying Squad	DSupt
12/5/69	C1	Murder Squad	DCS
14/3/71 Retired	Retired	32 years 8 m 16 days	Exemplary

CENTRAL RECORD OF SERVICE

D-5 (Records) No.

Rank: Pc C.I.D.   Name: Francis Arthur   Surname: WILLIAMS   Warrant No. 126,982

Former Warrant No.

M.P.-57-18050/Ex W196

DATE OF JOINING	DATE OF BIRTH	PLACE OF BIRTH	HEIGHT		PREVIOUS HISTORY			Decorations	Married or Single	No. of Children	TRANSFERS		
			Ft.	Ins.	Education	Occupation	Police or Other Public Service. Service in H.M. Forces and Period on Reserve				Date	Div.	Date
24.6.28	15/4/14	Ebbw Vale, Mon.	5	10¾	Elementary	Carpenter	R.A.C. attached 9 Commando d/Sgt 142241.758 22/7/42 to 27/11/46		M				

EXAMINATIONS

DURING PROBATIONARY PERIOD			EDUCATIONAL EXAMS. DURING SERVICE				TECHNICAL EXAMS.				SPECIAL EXAMS.		
Police Duty	Education	First Aid	2nd Class		1st Class		Uniform	C.I.D.	Passed	Failed	Type	Passed	Failed
			Passed	Failed	Passed	Failed							
Training School 100		P	28.7.39		13.4.4. Pro. 2.5.4.		Sergeant	Detective Branch Passed	14.12.46				

FIRST AID EXAMINATION

PROMOTIONS AND APPOINTMENTS

ADVANCEMENTS IN PAY

SERVICE AT A NAVAL OR MILITARY STATION FROM WHICH THE OFFICER WAS WITHDRAWN ON GENERAL REDUCTION OF ESTABLISHMENT

NAVAL STATION   FROM   TO   MILITARY STATION

REMOVAL AND CAUSE—PENSION

Resigned		
Discharged	On 14 March 1971	Lump Sum £5593.28
Pension	£2048.88	Commuted £484.71
Gratuity		H.O. Authority No. 56/19441 Date 17.3.71
R.D.K.		
Age on Retirement 53	Service 32 Years 8 Months 16 days	

No.		Amount	COMMENDATIONS AND AWARDS. By whom and for what Service	No.	Date of P.O.	REPORTS
			Comm: Devotion to duty while off duty. vigilance & ability case of shop breaking. 225/41/864.			
2	30.9.41		Comm: case of shopbreaking 225/41/1349.			
3	30.1.42		Comm: case of larceny & receiving. w.o.o. 200/41/5600			
4	18.4.44		Comm. For enterprise in a case of robbery. also commended at Clacton Magistrates Court. (W.O.O.) 202/44/95			
5	8.5.51		Comm: For ability and persistence in a case of burglary (w.o.o) 225/51/725.			
6	31.7.53		Comm: For keen observation and ability in case of conspiracy to defraud. W.O.O. 205/53/578.			
7	11.8.53		Comm: For ability and perseverance in a case of housebreaking. Also commended at the County of London Sessions 225/53/1081. W.O.O.			
	3.2.56		Comm: For ability and persistence in a case of conspiracy to steal. (w.o.o) 205/56/1095			
	25.5.56		Comm: For ability and determination in arresting a gang of violent criminals. (WAO) 202/56/210			
10	30.5.58		Comm: For ability and perseverance in a case of warehousebreaking. W.A.O.) 225/58/968			
11	4.10.60		Comm: For ability & persistence in a case of larceny & receiving. Also commended at the County of London Sessions (w.o.o) 202/60/549			
12	28.12.62		Comm: For determination + ability in arresting three active safe blowers. (W.O.O) 202/62/964			
13	29.1.63		Comm: For ability & persistence in arresting an organised gang of bank thieves (w.o.o) 225/62/1174			
14	10.5.63		Comm: For tenacity + ability resulting in a gang of armed + dangerous criminals being convicted of conspiracy to rob. (W.O.O.) 202/63/57.			

Stanley James MOORE
Born 28/5/27 Crediton, Devon 5'11 ¼"
Joined 27/9/48 Warrant Number 94/133857
Secondary Education and then Farm Student
Married with 2 children

Date	District	Borough	Promoted to:
27/9/48	TS	Training School	PC
10/1/49	X	Ealing	
11/10/54	D	Paddington	DC
1/9/60	E	Camden	DS(2)
15/5/61	C8	Flying Squad	
21/6/65	E	Camden	DS(1)
1/4/66	C8	Flying Squad	
16/10/67	E	Camden	DI
6/5/68	C11	Criminal Intelligence	
24/8/70	E	Camden	DCI
5/6/72	A10	Complaints	DSupt and DCS
26/8/75	C9	Metropolitan and Provincial Crime Branch	
Retired	Retired	29 years 297 days	Exemplary

Rank: Detective Inspector / (S.) Det. Chief Inspector / DET SUPT / P.C. (CID)
Christian Names: STANLEY JAMES
Surname: MOORE
Warrant No. 133851
National Insurance No. LW/89/54/61/A
Former Warrant No. 94/

PREVIOUS HISTORY

Date of Joining	Date of Birth	Place of Birth	Height (Feet/Inches)	Education	Occupation	Police or other Public Service, Service in H.M. Forces and Period of Reserve	Decorations	Married or Single / Sex / Date of Birth	No. of Children	Transfers (Date / Divn.)
27.9.48	28.5.27	Crediton Devon	5 11¼	Secondary	Farm Student	19102019 Sdr. R.A. 21.11.46 – 18.10.48	Police L.S. and G.C. Medal 9.9.58	G / 1/52 M	2	10.1.49 X 26.8.75; 11.10.54 D 26.8.75 C; 1.9.60; 15.8.61 CO.C8; 1.4.60 OO.(C.8); 6.5.62 (C.11)

Division to which Posted: T.S.

EXAMINATIONS

Entrance Exam.	4.24/6.50
Probationary Period Police Duty	
Training School	9/120
9 Months	T/100 Passed 28.3.63
18 Months	Passed P.O. 24.1.50
Appointment Confirmed	29.9.50

Educational Exam during Service: Result / Date 1st Class / 2nd Class — EXEMPT; Passed 2.2.62; Passed 29.2.60

Police Duty Examination — Qualifying: Passed 24.3.56 *; Passed 3.4.65

Special Exams — Motor driver: Passed 45.56 Class 5, 73; Motor cycle 4th 59 Passed 18; Mounted Bch. Oct 59 Med.

First Aid: 29.4.70 E; 6.72 A10

CRIMINAL INVESTIGATION DEPARTMENT
Date of Appointment: 11-10-5
P.O. 8-10
Confirmed: P.O.

PROMOTIONS AND APPOINTMENTS AND ADVANCEMENTS IN PAY

Date of Promotion	Sergeant 2nd Class C.I.D.	Stn. Sergeant or 1st Class C.I.D.	Inspector Uniform or 2nd Class C.I.D.	S.D. Inspector or 1st Class C.I.D.	Chief Inspector DET	Superintendent DET CHE SUPT	Commander
	1.9.60	Aug 21.6.65	16.10.6		24.3.70	7.5.73	17.9.73
	P.O. 30.8.60	P.O. 15.65	P.O. 6.10.6		13.7.70	4.5.73	14.9.73

WEEKLY 19.10.10 — MONTHLY P.P.R. 1973

Constable:
27.9.48 105/-
1.7.49 £6.6.6
2.10.50 £6.10.4
3 Aug 1951 £7.17.2
...

ELECTS TO UPDATE BACK SERVICE FROM 61%
By a) Reduction in pension
b) Lump sum
c) Increased pen. cons. 3-6

Central Service + V 209115 660 Payable by Home Office. O.97/73/428.
Selected to attend the Intermediate Course at Police College from 4.7.72 to 18.9.72

NOT eligible for allowance under Regn. 65(A)(2), P.R.R.

Selected to attend the Intermediate Command Course at the Police College from 4th July to 18th September P.O. 22.6.7

COMMENDATIONS

No.	Police Order	Commendations	Corres. No.
1.	18.6.54	Comm.: For courage and determination in arresting two violent criminals	W.A.O 885/54/770
2.	5.7.57	Comm.: For ability and initiative in effecting the arrest of three persistent criminals (W.A.O)	225/57/921
3.	6.12.57	Comm.: For ability and persistence in arresting eight men for shop breaking. Also commended at Birmingham Quarter Sessions. (W.O.O)	225/57/1814
4.	23.2.60	Comm.: For courage, tenacity in the arrest of a persistent thief for taking + driving away a motor car. Also commended at the County of London Sessions. (W.A.O)	224/59/3881
5.	4.8.61	Comm.: For ability and persistence in a case of murder. (W.O.O)	201/61/50
6.	29.1.63	Comm.: For ability, persistence in arresting an organised gang of bank thieves (W.O.O)	225/62/1719
7.	10.5.63	HIGHLY COMMENDED: Comm.: For outstanding courage + initiative resulting in a gang of armed and dangerous criminals being convicted of conspiracy to rob. (W.A.O)	302/63/37
	18.6.63	Awarded £20 from Bac St M.M.C. Reward Fund	303/63/37
8.	1.6.65	Comm.: For ability and perseverance in a case of robbery with violence. Also commended at the Crown court Manchester. (W.O.O)	202/64/1272
9.	13.7.65	Comm.:— For ability and persistence leading to the arrest of a gang of active criminals concerned in a serious case of robbery with violence. Also commended at the Central Criminal Court. (W.O.O)	202/65/260
10.	5.8.66	Comm.:— For ability and persevering conduct in the arrest and conviction of two active criminals for robbery with violence. (W.O.O)	202/66/580
11.	18.8.67	Comm.:— For perseverance and ability leading to the arrest and conviction of a persistent and troublesome criminal. Also commended at Hertford Assizes and by the Director of Public Prosecutions.	225/67/539

DRIVING RECORD
	Class	Date
Car: class	5	4/56
Autos		54
M/Cycle: class		
Traffic Patrol (std)		
Authorised Examiner		

REMOVAL AND CAUSE—PENSION

Resigned / Discharged / Died	On 14-8-77 APP 8360.060	Cause: Service Group 5519.17 Range 2-12418.14
Pension Gratuity	£4253.08	H.O. Authority No.	Date
Age at Retirement / Service	29 Years	294 Days

Certificate of Conduct: EXEMPLARY

M.P.-67328/3,000 June/1948 A27

RANK Det./Inspector	CHRISTIAN NAMES STANLEY. JAMES.		SURNAME MOORE	
WT. No. 133857	FORMER WT. No. 94.	NAT. INS. No. LW 50 61/5	DIV. No. C.I.D.	

DATE OF BIRTH	PLACE OF BIRTH	FORMER TRADE OR CALLING	DATE OF MARRIAGE	CHILDREN		CYCLIST	MOTOR DRIVING	
				SEX	DATE OF BIRTH		NATURE OF TEST	PASSED
28·5·27	CREDITON DEVON	FARM. STUDENT	4·9·54 M	G	16.2.65		CLASS 5. Re-test	4·5·56 2·11·67
DATE OF JOINING FORCE 27·9·48	HEIGHT 5 FT. 11¼ IN.							

WHISTLE No.	DECORATIONS	FIRST AID		WHETHER A SUBSCRIBER TO				
		DATE	CLASS	M.P. FR. SOCIETY	M.P.P.A.	ORPHANS	CON. HOME	ATH. CLUB
		" 48.	C.			YES.	YES.	YES.
		4·4·52.	V.					
LAMP No.		20·10·59	M.	WHETHER IN POSSESSION OF :—				
		2·2·66	Re-exam	GENERAL ORDERS (IF CO. COPY No.)			115 14154	
				CURRENT M.P. GUIDE				

ADDRESS	NAME, ADDRESS AND RELATIONSHIP OF PERSON TO BE COMMUNICATED WITH IN CASE OF EMERGENCY
23 Conway Gardens Sutting xiv 904 1556	

TRANSFERS			PROMOTIONS AND APPOINTMENTS			CIVIL DEFENCE		OTHER PUBLIC SERVICE AND PERIOD ON RESERVE

DATE	DIVN.	STN. CODE	DATE	DIVN.	STN. CODE	RANK	DATE	Respirator		
10.49	X	XH	24·8·70	L	G3			Helmet		19102010 BDR. R.A.
29·9·51	X	XD	5·6·72	CO	A10	P.C. (C.I.D.)	11·54	Gum Boots		21·11·46 TO 18·10·48.
11·10·54	D	PP.	26·9·73	CO	C·9.	P.S. or P.S. (2nd Cl.)	1960	Training	Date	
26.55	D	DP.				S.P.S. or P.S. (1st Cl.)	21·65	Part 1	"X"	
1960	E	ED				Inspector	16·10·67	Part 2	"X"	
1556	C8					Ch. Inspector	24·8·70			Class Cu. 1955/57
21·2·65	E	ED	Date and cause of leaving Force			Supt. (II)				9500·8··
1·4·66	CO	C·8.				Supt. (I)	7·5·73	Radius 1.	17'55	
16·10·67	E	ED								4·8·74
6·5·68	CO	C·11								

SPECIAL QUALIFICATIONS		EDUCATIONAL EXAMS. DURING SERVICE						POLICE DUTY EXAMINATIONS				
NATURE	PASSED	2ND CLASS		1ST CLASS		Probationers Exam. If over 85% marks at 15 mos. service	CLASS	COMPETITIVE		QUALIFYING	
		RESULT	DATE	RESULT	DATE			RESULT	DATE	RESULT	DATE
Mounted Branch											
Pistol Shooting		EXEMPT		Failed	PO 4662		P.S. or P.S. (2nd Class)			PASSED	24.3.56
Teleprinter				Failed	28.2.63						
Wireless		1		Passed	27.2.64						
Traffic Patrol							Station or P.S. (1st Class)				
Shorthand										Passed	3.4.65

No.	DATE OF P.O.	COMMENDATIONS AND AWARDS (Brief particulars only)	CORRES. No.	REMARKS
1	23·2·52	COMMANDER - robbery. W.A.D.	202/52/719	
2	5·53	COMMANDER - receiving W.A.D.		
3	9·54	COMMANDER - receiving W.A.D.	X/4/88	
4	18·54	COMMISSIONER - courage and determination - 2 violent criminals	225/54/770	Not entitled to removal expenses on Transfer to ED
5	5·7·57	COMMISSIONER - ABILITY & INITIATIVE ARRESTING 3 PERSISTENT CRIMINALS	225/57/921	

M.P.-54-53623/16M   W140

RANK Det. Ch/Supt	CHRISTIAN NAMES STANLEY JAMES		SURNAME MOORE	
WT. No. 133857	FORMER WT. No.	NAT. INS. No. LW 89 54 61 A	DIVN No. 'E'	

DATE OF BIRTH	PLACE OF BIRTH	FORMER TRADE OR CALLING	DATE OF MARRIAGE	CHILDREN		CYCLIST	MOTOR DRIVING	
				SEX	DATE OF BIRTH		NATURE OF TEST	PASSED
28.5.27	CREDITON	FARM		G	16.2.65		CLASS V	5.5.56
JOINING FORCE 27.9.48	DEVON HEIGHT 5 FT. 11¼ IN.	STUDENT	/					

DECORATIONS	OTHER PUBLIC SERVICE AND PERIOD ON RESERVE
	Bdr. - R.A. 19102010
	21.11.46 - 18.10.48.

TRANSFERS / PROMOTIONS AND APPOINTMENTS / SPECIAL QUALIFICATIONS

DATE	DIVN.	STN. CODE	DATE	DIVN.	STN. CODE	RANK	DATE	NATURE	PASSED	NATURE	PASSED
10.1.49	X	XH	5.6.72	CP	A10	P.C. (C.I.D.)	11.10.54	Mounted Branch			
29.10.51	X	XD	26.8.75	CO	C9	P.S. or P.S. (2nd Cl.)	1.9.60	Pistol Shooting			
11.10.54	D	DD				S.P.S. or P.S. (1st Cl.)	21.6.65	Teleprinter			
2.6.58	D	DP				Inspector C.D	14.10.67	Wireless			
1.9.60	E	ED				Ch. Inspector C.D	24.8.70	Traffic Patrol			
15.5.61	CO	C8				Supt.	7.5.73	Shorthand			
21.6.61	E	ED				Ch. Supt.	17.9.73				
1.4.66	CO	C8									
16.10.67	E	ED									
6.5.68	CO	C.11									
24.8.70	E	ED.									

ADDRESS 6 Woodlands		Date and cause of leaving Force
23 CONWAY GARDENS Road	WHETHER IN POSSESSION OF :—	
SOUTH KENTON Bushey, Kent	GENERAL ORDERS (IF SO, COPY No.)	
MIDDLESEX.	CURRENT M.P. GUIDE	

S.4/33 M.P.-66-78411/3M w145

FIRST AID		EDUCATIONAL EXAMS. DURING SERVICE					POLICE DUTY EXAMINATIONS				
DATE	CLASS	RESULT†	DATE	RESULT†	DATE	Probationers Exam. If over 85% marks at 15 mos. service.	CLASS	RESULT*	DATE	RESULT*	DATE
		LOWER	EXEMPT					QUAL	28.1.56		
		FAILED	1962				P.S. or P.S. (2nd Class)				
		FAILED	1963								
		HIGHER	1964					QUAL	3.4.65		
							Station or P.S. (1st Class)				
		* Higher, Lower or Failed						†Passed (Competitive), Qualified or Failed			

No.	DATE OF P.O.	COMMENDATIONS AND AWARDS (Brief particulars only)	CORRES. No.	REMARKS
		COMMISSIONERS		
		ELEVEN (11)		
		MINOR COMMENDATIONS.		
		EIGHT (8)		

D2/34

NAME: MOORE Stanley   Divl. No. ....

RANK: Det.Ch.Supt   Warrant No. 94/133857

PLACE OF BIRTH: Crediton Devon

Date of Joining	Date of Transfer to Station	HEIGHT ft. / ins.	PUBLIC SERVICE	FORMER TRADE OR CALLING
27.9.48	26.8.75	5 / 11¼		Farm Student
		Date of Birth 28.5.27		

M. or S.	No. of children	CYCLIST	FIRST AID CERT. Date	Class	MOTOR DRIVING Nature of Test	Passed
M	2		11.48	C		
			4.1.52	V		
			20.10.59	M		

ADDRESS (If Police Quarters state nature, e.g., Section House; Flat over Station; Receiver's House; Private House, etc.)

6 Woodlands Road,
Bushey Herts.

Name, address and relationship of person to be communicated with in case of emergency

1. Wife - s/a
2. Brother - F Moore, 59 Woodstock Rd Worcester

M.P.-71-85753/3M   D65

DIVISIONAL RECORD OF SERVICE   S.4 (Records) No. 31

Rank: Supt   Christian Names: STANLEY JAMES   Surname: MOORE   Divl. No. 468   Warrant No. 13...

National Insurance No. LW/83/54/61/A

DATE OF JOINING	DATE OF BIRTH	PLACE OF BIRTH	HEIGHT Ft. / Ins.	PREVIOUS HISTORY Education	Occupation	Police or Other Public Service. Service in H.M. Forces and Period on Reserve.	Decorations	Date of Marriage	CHILDREN Sex / Date of Birth	STATION CODE
27.9.48	28.5.27	Crediton Devon	5 / 11½	Secondary	Farm Student	19107010 Met. R.N. 21-11-46 - 18-10-48	L.S&G.C. 5.3.71	M 9.54 / 8	G 16.2.66 B.	
T.S.										

LAMP No. 22552

EXAMINATIONS

Probationers Exam. If over 60% marks at 15 mos. service	EDUCATIONAL EXAMS. DURING SERVICE 2nd Class Result / Date	1st Class Result / Date		POLICE DUTY EXAMINATIONS Class	COMPETITIVE Result / Date	QUALIFYING Result / Date	Result / Date	MOTOR DRIVING Nature of Test	Passed	FIRST AID Date / Class / Date / Cl.
EXEMPT.		FAILED 10.4.62 FAILED 28.2.63 Passed 27.2.64	Sergeant or 2nd Class (C.I.D.) Sergt.		Passed 28.1.66			Class V (G.P.Cars) 18.5.50	5.5.50	11.48 / C / 4.1.52 / passed / 20.10.59 / M / 2.2.66 / R
			Station or 1st Class (C.I.D.) Sergt.		Failed 3.4.65					

PROMOTIONS AND APPOINTMENTS Uniform / Date	C.I.D. / Date	WHETHER A SUBSCRIBER TO M.P.P.A. Tables	M.P. Friendly Society Tables	Orphans' Fund	Athletics	Date / Divl. / Divl. No.
Sergeant	Constable 11.10.54	1ca	1ca	1ca		10.1.59 C
Stn. or Clk. Sergt.	2nd Cl. Sergeant 1.9.60					20.10.51 C
Inspector	1st Cl. Sergeant 21.6.65					1.10.55 CD
S.D. or Dist. Insp.	2nd Cl. Inspector 16.10.67	WHETHER IN POSSESSION OF :—				2.9.60 CD
Ch. Inspector	1st Cl. Inspector 24.8.70	GENERAL ORDERS (if so, Copy No.) NO H494	CURRENT M.P. GUIDE			1.9.60 CD
Superintendent	Ch. Inspector 17.5.73	1st Special Increment				21.6.65 CD
Dy. Commander	Superintendent Dy. Commander 17.9.73	1st Additional Increment				1.6.66 CO-CD
under	Commander	2nd				6.5.68 CD

CIVIL DEFENCE

	DATE	ADDRESS		Nature	Passed	SPECIAL QUALIFICATIONS Nature	Passed
Part 1 Completed	1 x Div.	6 Woodlands Road	Mounted Branch				
Part 2 Completed	2 x Div. 5/26	Bushey, Herts.	Pistol Shooting	10.8.61			
RANK N			Teleprinter				
BLOOD 10			Wireless				
STEEL HELMET 7			Traffic Patrol				
Respirator Shattered	17-1-58		Shorthand				

No.	Date of P.O.	Amount	COMMENDATIONS AND AWARDS. By whom and for what Service	Corres. No.	No.	Date of P.O.	MISCONDUCT REPORTS — COMMENDATIONS	Punishment Corres No.
1.	23.2.52		*both III* - For initiative and keenness in case of robbery. (W.A.O.)	202/52/79			(re last commend:-) Awarded £20 from Bow Street Metropolitan Magistrates' Court Reward Fund. (P.O. 18.6.63 corres. 202/63/27)	
2.	9.4.53		COMMANDER II - for keenness, attention to duty in case of receiving and housebreaking (W.A.O.)		14	1.6.65	Commissioner - For ability and perseverance in a case of robbery with violence. Also commended at Bow Court, Manchester.	W.O.O.
3	9.6.54		Commander II, for ability in a case of receiving (W.A.O.)	X/4/55.				
4	18.6.54		Commissioner - courage & determination in arresting two violent criminals (W.A.O.)	225/54/70	15	12.7.65	Commissioner - For ability and persistence leading to the arrest of a gang of active criminals concerned in a serious case of robbery with violence. Also commended at C.C.C. (W.O.O.)	202/65/260
5.	5.7.57		Commissioner - for ability and initiative in effecting the arrests of 3 persistent criminals	225/57/92				
6	6.12.57		Commissioner - For ability and persistence in arresting 8 men for theft. Also commended at Birmingham Quarter Sess. (W.O.O.)	225/57/94	16	5.8.66	Commissioner - For ability and perseverance resulting in the arrest & conviction of two active criminals for robbery with violence. W.O.O.	202/66/582
7	28.3.58	–	Commander II - For initiative & determination in arresting 3 agents for housebreaking. (W.A.O.)	230/58/393	17	24.10.66	Commander - For perseverance and ability resulting in the arrest and conviction of an expert team of jewel thieves. (W.O.O.)	231/66/2009
8	29.7.58		Commander - for detective ability & good team work in the arrest of three housebreakers and two receivers. W.O.O.	228/58/2	76			
9	12.2.60		Commander II. for persistence & initiative in an involved investigation case of storebreaking.	220/59/619	18	30.5.67	COMMANDER II - For zeal and tenacity leading to the arrest and conviction of three active criminals for receiving. (W.O.O.)	230/67/5158
10	23.7.60.		Commissioner - for courage and tenacity in the arrest of a persistent thief for taking and driving away a motor car. Also Commended at C.L.S. (W.A.O.)	229/60/3881.	19	18.9.67	Commissioner - For perseverance and ability leading to the arrest and conviction of a persistent and troublesome criminal. Also commended at Hertford Assizes and by the Director of Public Prosecutions.	231/67/537
	x/8/61		COMMISSIONER - FOR ABILITY AND PERSISTENCE in a case of murder. (W.O.O.)	201/61/50				
	29.1.63		FOR ABILITY AND PERSISTENCE IN ARRESTING AN ORGANISED GANG OF BANK THIEVES (W.O.O.)	225/62/719				
			COMMISSIONER — HIGHLY COMMENDED for sustaining courage and initiative resulting in a ... of armed and dangerous criminals being arrested conspiracy... (W.A.O.)	202/63/27				

'nder P.O.
12-8-75.

TRANSFER
BACK 'E' Division
26/8/75

Seconded to the Home Office
Number at H.O. is 828-9848
ext 129.

Chief Superintendent's Office,
Albany Street Station.

.......22nd. June.......1965

G.O. Sec. 6, para 110 - 112
Sec. 2/64

TRAVELLING AND REMOVAL EXPENSES

On being transferred to 'E' Division, this officer was granted "special" permission not to move. He has been informed that he will not be entitled to travelling or removal expenses if he subsequently moves.

P.S. (1) CID/133857 MOORE (ED).

Divisional Superintendent ---
Chief Superintendent 'E'

James Francis NEVILL Q.P.M.
Born 20/2/27 St Marylebone 6'0"
Joined 22/11/48 Warrant Number 25/134079
Higher Grade Elementary Education and then Driver
Married with 2 children

Date	District	Borough	Promoted to:
22/11/48	TS	Training School	PC
7/3/49	A	Westminster	
10/5/54	C4	Criminal Record Office	DC
3/10/55	V	Kingston	
21/12/59	W	Wandsworth	DS(2)
6/2/61	B	Kensington	
7/1/63	C8	Flying Squad	DS(1)
1/4/65	A	Westminster	DI
21/6/65	B	Kensington	
1/5/67	T	Richmond	DCI
4/9/67	C	Westminster	DSupt in 1968?
8/4/69 -21/6/69	Bramshill	Intermediate Command Course	
21/7/69	C5	C.I.D. Correspondence	DCS
4/10/71	A	Westminster	
1/1/74	C1	Murder Squad	
1/3/76	C13	Anti Terrorism Squad	Commander
4/1/79	4HQ	S.E. London H.Q.	
11/1/80	Barbados	Barbados	
26/3/80	Return to M.P.	Return to M.P.	
31/12/80 Retired	Retired	32 years 40 days	Exemplary

CENTRAL RECORD OF SERVICE

Rank: Commander (C.I.D.) **Christian Names:** JAMES FRANCIS **Surname:** NEVILL O.P.M. **Warrant No.** 134079

National Insurance No. AA/59/02/71/B

DATE OF JOINING	DATE OF BIRTH	PLACE OF BIRTH	HEIGHT FEET/INCHES	PREVIOUS HISTORY				MARRIED or SINGLE	No. OF CHILDREN		TRANSFERS			
				EDUCATION	OCCUPATION	POLICE OR OTHER PUBLIC SERVICE, SERVICE IN H.M. FORCES AND PERIOD OF RESERVE	DECORATIONS		SEX	DATE of BIRTH	DATE	DIVN.	DATE	DIVN.
22.11.48	20.2.27	St. Marylebone	6 0	Elementary (Higher Grade)	Driver	1948/06 R.A.F Q.O.K.W.K 27.11.45 – 26.5.48	Q.P.M. F.O. 25.5.71	M	B	G	7.3.49 A	A 4.10.71 A. 10.5.54 C 1.1.74 C.1 3.10.55 W 1376 C.13 21.12.59 B 7.09 NO.6 6.2.61 C.8 1.4.65 A 21.6.65

EXAMINATIONS

ENTRANCE EXAM	325/650	EDUCATIONAL EXAM DURING SERVICE		POLICE DUTY EXAMINATION					SPECIAL EXAMS		FIRST AID		CRIMINAL INVESTIGATION DEPARTMENT
PROBATIONARY PERIOD Police Duty	120/120												DATE OF APPOINTMENT P.O. 5.54
TRAINING SCHOOL													P.O. 7.5.54
9 MONTHS	94/100												CONFIRMED P.O. 7.6.55
15 MONTHS	Passed												
APPOINTMENT CONFIRMED	28.11.50												

PROMOTIONS AND APPOINTMENTS AND ADVANCEMENTS

DATE OF PROMOTION	SERGEANT 2ND CLASS C.I.D.	SERGEANT 1st CLASS C.I.D.	INSPECTOR Uniform or 2nd Class C.I.D.	S.D. INSPECTOR or 1st Class C.I.D.	CHIEF INSPECTOR	SUPERINTENDENT	DEPUTY COMMANDER	COMMANDER
	21.12.59 P.O. 18.12.59	7.1.63 P.O. 4.1.63	21.3.65 P.O. 23.3.65		1.5.69 P.O. 12.4.69	21.7.69 (Temp) P.O. 18.7.69		1.7.76 P.O. 29.6.76

COMMENDATIONS

No.	Police Order	COMMENDATIONS
1.	16.9.52	Comm'r. for determination in effecting the arrest of a violent criminal. (W.O.O.)
2.	25.9.53	Commr. for ability in effecting the arrest of a desirable and persistent thief. W.P.O. 230/53/2615.
3.	1.4.58	Commr. for ability and persistence in a case of conspiracy to forge and utter bank notes. (W.O.O.) 336/57/596
1.	6.1.78	New Years Honours 1978 – Her Majesty the Queen has been graciously pleased to award Commander Nevill the Queens Police Medal.

REMOVAL AND CAUSE—PENSION

			CAUSE	Service
RESIGNED		on 31-12-80	Gross pen	10623.825
			Lump Sum	34805.84
PENSION	£ 7792.58		Reduction	233.724
AGE ON RETIREMENT	53	SERVICE 32	YEARS 40	DAYS

CERTIFICATE OF CONDUCT Exemplary

M.P-9753R/3,000 June/1948 A37

APP'd 1975/

Car + Van	18.7.51
GP + Van	17.4.53
GP (u/a) Class 5	1.11.55
GP Class 5	11.5.65
Automatics	3.6.68

Thomas Albert THORBURN
Born 4/10/24 North Kensington 5'11"
Joined 17/7/50 Warrant Number 68/135965
Elementary Education and then Fitter
Married with 2 children

Date	District	Borough	Promoted to:
17/7/50	TS	Training School	PC
6/11/50	M	Southwark	
18/2/52	K	Barking	
27/2/56	C4	Criminal Record Office	DC
16/4/56	K	Barking	
10/9/62	C8	Flying Squad	
4/5/64	H	Hackney	DS(2)
10/1/66	RCS	Regional Crime Squad	
1/5/68	C12	Regional Crime Squad	
24/8/70	K	Barking	
16/7/75 Retired	Retired	25 years 0 days	Exemplary

No.	Police Order	COMMENDATIONS	Corres.	No.	Police Order	REPORTS
1.	13.4.54	Commd. For initiative and persistence in arresting a gang of troublesome housebreakers. Also commended at Stratford Magistrates Court. W.O.O. 225/54/22.				
2	11.3.55	Commd:- For initiative and ability in arresting two active shopbreakers. Also commended at Stratford Magistrate Court. (W.A.O.) 205/54/2370				
3.	8.11.55	Commd:- For ability and perseverance in arresting a troublesome criminal (W.O.O) 230/55/2758				
4.	15.8.58	Commd:- For valuable assistance in a case of murder. (W.O.O) 201/58/165				
5.	3.7.59	Commd. For valuable assistance in a case of murder. (W.O.O) 201/59/75				
6.	8.1.65	Commd:— For persistence & ability in effecting the arrest of a team of active lorry thieves 230/64/249.				
7	1.6.68	Commd. For persistence and detective ability resulting in the arrest and conviction of three dangerous criminals for shopbreaking and forcing safes with explosives (W.O.O) 225/68/106				

R.L.A//N.E.
2 4 SEP 1975

REMOVAL AND CAUSE—PENSION

Resigned			Cause	Service
Discharged	On 16.7.75		1692 440	
Dead	Amt £ 3183·87 £ 3384 880		18.335	44-34A 118 343
Pension	£ 1262.67			
Gratuity	£ 1181·98?	H.O. Authority No.	Date	
R—D's			Corres. No.	
Age on Retirement	50	Service	25 Years	0 Days /
Certificate of Conduct	EXEMPLARY			

M.P.-41700/3,000 Feb./1950 A57

A.3/R/34

NAME	THORBURN, Thomas Albert		Divl. No. C.I.D.	PLACE OF BIRTH
RANK	P.S.2.	Warrant No. 68/135965		North Kensington

Date of Joining	Date of Transfer to Station	HEIGHT		PUBLIC SERVICE	FORMER TRADE OR CALLING
		ft.	ins.		
17.7.50	4.5.64.	5 Date of Birth 4.10.24	11	R.A.C 6298676 L/CPL 27.10.41 – 31.7.46	Fitter

M. or S.	No. of children	CYCLIST	FIRST AID CERT.		MOTOR DRIVING	
			Date	Class	Nature of Test	Passed
M	2		Sept.50 Apr.53. 28.4.59	C V Med	Class.5.	13.10.58

ADDRESS (If Police Quarters state nature, e.g. Section House; Flat over Station; Receiver's House; Private House; etc.)

Name, Address and Relationship of Person to be Communicated with in case of Emergency

Wife S/A

S.4/34 M.P.-62-70795/4,800 w150 (2)

John Kenneth SLIPPER
Born 20/4/24 Ealing 6'3"
Joined 30/4/51 Warrant Number 19/136886
Elementary Education and then Electrician
Married with 2 children

Date	District	Borough	Promoted to:
30/4/51	TS	Training School	PC
13/8/51	T	Richmond	
3/12/51	B	Kensington	
7/5/56	T	Richmond	DC
4/11/57	F	Hammersmith	
8/9/58	T	Richmond	
1/1/62	C8	Flying Squad	DS(2) DS(1) 31/3/64 DI 11/7/66
8/1/67	Q	Harrow	DCI 2/9/68
4/10/71	C10	Stolen Vehicle Squad	DCS
5/3/73	C8	Flying Squad	
4/1/77	Q	Harrow	Uniform CS
24/12/79 Retired	Retired	28 years 239 days	Exemplary

~~Detective Inspector~~ ~~CH Insp.~~ ~~P.S. (2nd class C.I.D.)~~ ~~Det~~ CH Superintendent.

CENTRAL RECORD OF SERVICE

M.P. (Records) No. 36.

Rank ~~P.S. (C.I.D.)~~ Christian Names JOHN KENNETH Surname SLIPPER Warrant No. 136886

National Insurance No. AX-68-31-47-D

Former Warrant No.

Date of Joining	Date of Birth	Place of Birth	Height Feet	Height Inches	Previous History: Education	Occupation	Police or other Public Service, Service in H.M. Forces and Period on Reserve	Decorations	Married or Single	No. of Children: Sex	Date of Birth
30.[illegible] Division to which Posted [illegible]	20.4.24	Ealing London.	6.	3.	Elementary	Fireman Electrician	1285220 L.A.C. R.A.F. 23.4.41 – 6.3.46	Police L.S. and G.C. Medal 20.14.9.73	M.	G G	2.9.55 20.7.57

Transfers

Date	Divn.
13.8.51	T.
3.12.51	B
7.5.56	T
4.11.[illegible]	F
8.9.58	T
1.1.62	C8
8.1.67	Q
4.10.71	CO (CID)
5.3.73	C8
4.1.77	Q

EXAMINATIONS

		Educational Exam. During Service: 2nd Class Result	2nd Class Date	1st Class Result	1st Class Date
Entrance Exam.	378/650				
Probationary Period Police Duty					
Training School	120/120	EXEMPT		Passed	10.2.55
9 Months	Good.				
15 Months	PASSED OVER 85% P.O. [illegible]				
Appointment Confirmed	P.O. 5-5-53				

Police Duty Examination

Class	Competitive Result	Competitive Date	Qualifying Result	Qualifying Date	Result	Date
Sergeant or 2nd Class (C.I.D.) Sergt.			Passed	20.1.57 *		
Station or 1st Class (C.I.D.) Sergt.			Passed	19.1.63 ⓢ		

Special Exams.

Type	Passed	Failed
~~Motor driver~~	~~Class 2 (7.8.57)~~	
Motor cycle		
Mounted Bch.		
Wireless R.T.		
Traffic Patrol		
Teleprinter		
PISTOLS	2.8.63	

First Aid

Date	Result
TS.	Passed
3.6.[illegible]	Voucher
21.4.60	Medal

Criminal Investigation Department

Date of Appointment	7.5.56 P.O. 4.5.56
Confirmed	P.O. 4.6.57

PROMOTIONS AND APPOINTMENTS AND ADVANCEMENTS IN PAY

Date of Promotion	Sergeant 2nd Class C.I.D.	PS ~~Stn. Sergeant or~~ 1st Class C.I.D.	Inspector Uniform or 2nd Class C.I.D.	Chief Inspector	Superintendent	Chief Superintendent	Deputy Commander	Commander
	16.4.62	31.3.64	Tog. 11.7.66	2.9.68	~~4~~	4.10.71		
	P.O. 13.4.62	P.O. 24.3.64	P.O. 8.7.66. Sub. 10.10.66 P.O. 4.10.66	P.O. 16.8.68 Subs. 24.2.69 P.O. 18.2.69	P.O.	P.O. 28.9.71 Sub. 23.5.72 P.O. 19.5.72.	P.O.	P.O.

Weekly

Constable		Sergeant		1st Class		Inspector		Chief Inspector	
[illegible]		16.4.62	19.14.10	31.3.64	£23.5.9.	11.7.66	£122.10.0	~~2.9.68~~	~~145.16.8~~
		1.9.62	20.8.3	1.9.64	24.18.4	~~11.7.67~~	~~126.8.4~~	2.2.63	153.6.8
3 AUG 1951	7.13.4	1.2.63	20.17.10	1.1.66	25.17.6	1.3.67	133.6.8	1.9.69	157.13.4
4.5.53	7.17.2	16.4.63	21.13.2	31.3.66	26.14.9	11.7.67	137.10.–	2.4.69	162.13.4
14.[illegible].54	8.14.5	16.4.64	22.8.6			11.7.68	141.13.4	1.1.70	176.5.0
[illegible]	[illegible]							2.9.70	192.1.8
[illegible]	[illegible]								
8.16.12.55	10.16.7								
30.4.56	[illegible]								
1.2.[illegible]	11.[illegible]								
6.[illegible]	11.[illegible]								
[illegible]	12.3.5								
5.3.58	12.[illegible]								
2.3.59	13.18.[illegible]								
2.3.60	13.6.3								
1.4.60	17.8.10								

Monthly

ⓢ Allowance paid under Regn. 40. P.R. 1952.

C P.P.R. 1956 (NEW SCHEME [illegible] PENSION) NO REDUCTION [illegible] PENSION Pen. Cons. [illegible] plus addl. cons. 0-2% Less 1s 2d. p.w.

Miscellaneous Notes * Transferred to uniform duty for 31-78 P.O. 13.12.77. Stn. of service until 31.12.79 P.O. 7/78/2221

* NOT eligible for allowance under Regn. 40 (A) (2), P.R. 1952

No.	Police Order	Commendations	Corres.
1.	12.10.52	Commd. for devotion to duty while off duty and ability in the arrest of the persistent criminals. Also commended at Epping Magistrates Court.	220/52/3123
	8.11.65	Commd:— for initiative and ability leading to the arrest of a gang of violent criminals for conspiracy to rob (W.O.C.)	202/65/196
	7.1.66	Commd.— for ability and persistence leading to the arrest of a number of persons for aiding an escape from one of the Prisons. (W.O.C.)	53/65/256
	23.9.66	Commd.— for courage and devotion to duty in effecting the arrest of three vicious criminals for malicious shooting, one of whom was in possession of a loaded firearm, whereby PS Carr sustained personal injury. Also Commended at Chelmsford Assizes. (W.O.C.)	16/66/880

No.	Police Order	Reports

APPT 17.10.56.

Q	15.10.56
5	16.1.68

SPECTACLES

REMOVAL AND CAUSE—PENSION

Resigned ~~Discharged~~ ~~Died~~ On 24-12-79 APP 12,626.958 ORD. Cause Service + AGE

Pension Gratuity R.D's. £ 7851.78. H.O. Authority No. Date

Corres. No.

Age on Retirement 55 Service 28 Years 239 Days

Certificate of Conduct Exemplary

M.P.-4.70G/2,000 Feb./1950 A27

Louis Harry VAN DYKE
Born 3/3/29 South St Pancras 5'11¾"
Joined 10/3/52 Warrant Number ??/137728
Elementary Education and then Production Inspector
Married with 2 children

Date	District	Borough	Promoted to:
10/3/52	TS	Training School	PC
16/6/52	G	Hackney	
5/10/53	K	Barking	
23/3/59	H	Tower Hamlets	DC
7/8/62	E	Camden	
1/7/63	C8	Flying Squad	DS(2)
1/12/66	H	Hackney	DS(1)
25/8/69	D9	Detective Training School	DI
3/1/72	G	Shoreditch	
18/12/72	C9	Metropolitan and Provincial Crime Branch	DCI
9/9/74	J	Leyton	
2/6/75	A10	Complaints	DSupt
1/6/77	CIB(2)	Complaints	DCS
19/9/77	Y	Tottenham	
10/4/78	D9	Detective Training School	
14/1/80	K	Barking	
28/7/82 Retired on ill health pension	Retired on ill health pension	30 years 141 days	Exemplary

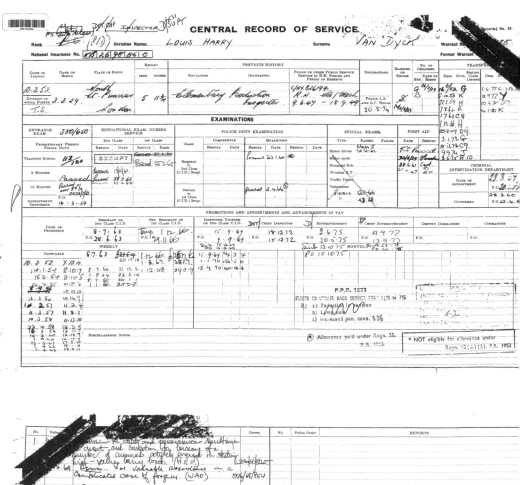

CENTRAL RECORD OF SERVICE

Rank	DET. CHF. Inspector	Christian Names	LOUIS HARRY	Surname	VAN DYCK	Warrant No.	

National Insurance No. WB 26 98 86 C

DATE OF JOINING	DATE OF BIRTH	PLACE OF BIRTH	HEIGHT	PREVIOUS HISTORY				DECORATIONS	MARRIED OR SINGLE	No. OF CHILDREN	TRANSFER
			FEET	INCHES	EDUCATION	OCCUPATION	POLICE OR OTHER PUBLIC SERVICE, SERVICE IN H.M. FORCES AND PERIOD AND PERIOD OF RESERVE				

Body table (reconstructed):

					PREVIOUS HISTORY					
10.3.52	3.3.29	North St. Pancras London	5	11¾	Elementary	Production Inspector	C/HX 826194. R.N. sto/mech 9.6.47 – 18.9.49	Police L.S. and G.C. Medal 20.8.74	G 4/7/39	

EXAMINATIONS

ENTRANCE EXAM.	380/650	EDUCATIONAL EXAM. DURING SERVICE		POLICE DUTY EXAMINATION					SPECIAL EXAMS.			FIRST AID	

Promotions section:

DATE OF PROMOTION	SERGEANT OR 2ND CLASS C.I.D.	STN. SERGEANT OR 1ST CLASS C.I.D.	INSPECTOR UNIFORM OR 2ND CLASS C.I.D.	CHIEF INSPECTOR	SUPERINTENDENT	CHIEF SUPERINTENDENT	DEPUTY COMMANDER	COMMANDER
	8.7.63 P.O. 28.6.63	Temp 1.12.66 P.O. 29.11.66	15.9.69 P.O. 9.9.69	18.12.72 P.O. 15.12.72	2.6.75 P.O. 30.5.75	9.9.77 P.O. 13.9.77		

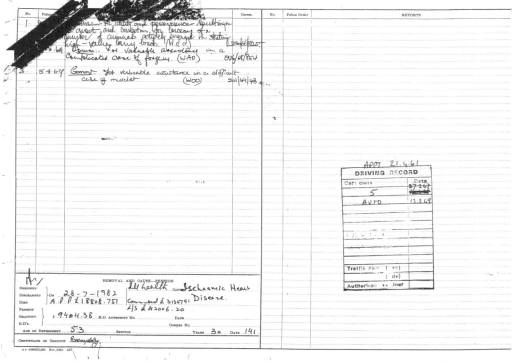

No.	5.8.69	Comm. for valuable assistance in a difficult case of murder (WOO) 201/69/43

DRIVING RECORD

Car. Class	Date
5	27.2.67
AUTO	13.2.69

Traffic Pat. (rd)

Authorised iner

REMOVAL AND CAUSE—PENSION

RESIGNED		
DISCHARGED	On 28-7-1982	Cause Ill health Ischaemic Heart Disease.
DIED	A.P.P. £18808.757 Commuted £3134791	
PENSION		L/S £42006.20
GRATUITY	£9404.38	H.O. AUTHORITY No.
R.D's.		CORRES. No.
AGE ON RETIREMENT	53	SERVICE YEARS 30 DAYS 141
CERTIFICATE OF CONDUCT	Exemplary	

NAT. HEALTH CCK/04/32/06 ✗   A.3/R/34

NAME VAN DYCK Louis Harry   Divl. No. C.I.D. | PLACE OF BIRTH
RANK P.C.   Warrant No. 137728 | ST. PANCRAS

Date of Joining	Date of Transfer to Station	HEIGHT ft.	HEIGHT ins.	PUBLIC SERVICE	FORMER TRADE OR CALLING
10/3/52	7/8/62	6	0	Royal Navy	Production Inspector
		Date of Birth 3/3/29		1947 - 49.	

M. or S.	No. of children	CYCLIST	FIRST AID CERT. Date	FIRST AID CERT. Class	MOTOR DRIVING Nature of Test	MOTOR DRIVING Passed
M.		YES.	May 52.	Red Hse	Class 5.	

ADDRESS (If Police Quarters state nature, e.g. Section House; Flat over Station; Receiver's House; Private House; etc.)

1 Durham House, Durham Rd

1 Rd.

Name, Address and Relationship of Person to be Communicated with in case of Emergency

TRANS. To c.g.c.8.
vide P.O.18 of 31.63.

S.4/34 M.P.-60-66214/4,800 W150 (2)

Would you please note that the officers shown on
the attached lists have elected to be members of No. 3
District Sports Club instead of No. 1 District Sports
Club and arrangements have been made for this to become
effective forthwith.   No. 1 District Sports Club will
pay their subscriptions quarterly to No. 3 District
Sports Club for the time being.   The question of this
being dealt with by S.4 Branch is still under consideration.
If any of the officers are transferred out of C.O. the
Secretaries and Treasurers of No. 1 and No. 3 District
Sports Clubs are to be notified accordingly.

A. Townsend

Commander 'A'

References

Books

Biggs, Ronald (1995). *Keep on Running.* (Bloomsbury Publishing PLC). ISBN-13: 978-0747521884

Biggs, Ronnie (1981). *Ronnie Biggs: His Own Story.* (Sphere). ISBN-13: 978-0722116371

Biggs, Michael and Silver, Neil (2002). *The Biggs Time: Ronnie and Michael – Man and Boy.* (Virgin Books). ISBN-13: 978-1852279882

Biggs, Ronnie and Pickard, Chris (2011). *Ronnie Biggs: Odd Man Out – The Last Straw.* (M Press (Media) Ltd). ISBN-13: 978-0957039827

Clarkson, Wensley. (2006). *Killing Charlie: The Bloody, Bullet-Riddled Hunt for the Most Powerful Great Train Robber of All.* (Mainstream Publishing). ISBN-13: 978-1845960353

Coates, Tim (2003). *The Great British Train Robbery, 1963.* (Tim Coates Publishing). ISBN-13: 978-1843810223

Cook, Andrew (2013). *The Great Train Robbery: The Untold Story from the Closed Investigation Files.* (The History Press Ltd). ISBN-13: 978-0752499819

Cox, Barry and Shirley, John and Short, Martin (1977). *The Fall of Scotland Yard.* (Penguin Books Ltd). ISBN-13: 978-0140523188

Delano, Anthony (2008). *Slip-Up: How Fleet Street caught Ronnie Biggs and Scotland Yard lost him: the story behind the scoop.* (Revel Barker). ISBN-13: 978-0955823831

Fewtrell, Malcolm (1964). *The Train Robbers.* (Barker). ASIN: B0000CMAIL

Fordham, Peta (1968). *The Robbers' Tale: The Real Story Of The Great Train Robbery.* (Penguin). ASIN: B0000CO873.

Foreman, Freddie. (2009). *Freddie Foreman: The Godfather of British Crime.* (John Blake Publishing Ltd). ISBN-13: 978-1844546893

Gosling John. (1965). *Great Train Robbery the Inside Story.* (Corgi Books). ASIN: B004OGY30Y

Gray, Mike and Currie, Tel (2011). *Ronnie Biggs: The Inside Story.* (Apex Publishing Ltd). ASIN: B004MMERWE

Guttridge, Peter (2008). *The Great Train Robbery.* (The National Archives). ISBN-13: 978-1905615322

Hatherill, George (1971). *A Detective's Story.* (McGraw-Hill). ISBN-13: 978-0070270251

Haugen, Brenda (1975). *The Great Train Robbery: History-Making Heist.* (Compass Point Books). ISBN-13: 978-0756543600

Kirby, Dick (2012). *The Guv'nors; Ten of Scotland Yard's Greatest Detectives.* (Wharncliffe). ASIN: B00APL5QS0

Mackenzie, Colin (1975). *Most Wanted Man: Story of Ronald Biggs.* (HarperCollins). ISBN-13: 978-0246108340

Millen, Ernest (1972). *Specialist in Crime.* (George G.Harrap). ASIN: B00BJN4LCA

Morris, J. (2013). *The Great Train Robbery: A New History.* (Amberley Publishing). ISBN-13: 978-1445606828

Read, Piers Paul (2013). *The Train Robbers: Their Story.* (Virgin Books). ISBN-13: 978-0753541760

Reynolds, Bruce (2000). *The Great Train Robbery Files* (Abstract Sounds Publishing). ISBN-13: 978-0953572465

Reynolds, Bruce (2003). *Crossing The Line The Autobiography of A Thief.* (Virgin Books). ISBN-13: 978-1852279295

Reynolds, Bruce and Biggs, Ronnie and Reynolds, Nick and Pickard, Christopher. (2013). *The Great Train Robbery 50th Anniversary: 1963-2013.* (M Press (Media) Ltd). ISBN-13: 978-0957255975

Reynolds, Bruce. (2011). *The Autobiography of a Thief: The Man Behind The Great Train Robbery.* (Virgin Books). ISBN-13: 978-0753539170

Richards, Ross (1964). *The Great Train Robbery.* (Consul). ASIN: B000S35WU2

Richardson, Charlie and Long, Bob (1992). *My Manor: An Autobiography.* (Pan Books) ISBN-13: 978-0330324007

Richardson, Eddie (2006). *The Last Word: My Life as a Gangland Boss.* (Headline). ISBN-13: 978-0755314010

Russell-Pavier, Nick and Richards, Stewart (2013). *Great Train Robbery: Crime of the Century: The Definitive Account.* (Phoenix). ISBN-13: 978-0753829264

Ryan Robert (2010). *Signal Red.* (Headline Review). ISBN-13: 978-0755358205

Sandbrook, Dominic (2009). *White Heat: A History of Britain in the Swinging Sixties 1964-1970.* (Abacus). ISBN-13: 978-0349118208

Sandbrook, Dominic (2010). *Never Had It So Good: A History of Britain from Suez to the Beatles.* (Abacus). ISBN-13: 978-0349115306

Slipper, Jack (1981). *Slipper of the Yard.* (Pan Macmillan) ISBN-13: 978-0283987021

Wheen, Francis (1982). *The Sixties.* (Century). ISBN-13: 978-0712600187

Williams, Frank (1973). *No Fixed Address.* (W.H. Allen). ISBN-13: 978-0491005241

Wisbey, Marilyn (2002). *Gangster's Moll.* (Time Warner Paperbacks). ISBN-13: 978-0751529753

Woodley, Len (2010). *Photocop: The Man Who Photographed the Great Train Robbery.* (Armadillo). ISBN-13: 978-0956544636

TV, Film and Video

Buster – Movie Connections (2009) by BBC Television

Buster (1988) by Hemdale Film Corp.

Days That Shook The World – The Great Train Robbery (2004) by Lion Television/ BBC Scotland/ History Channel

Die Gentlemen bitten zur Kasse (1966) by NDR

Great Crimes and Trials of the 20th Century (1993) Uden Associates

I married a Great Train Robber (1996) by Cutting Edge/ Channel 4

I was a Great Train Robber (2001) by Carlton TV/ Fulcrum Productions/ ITV4

Kidnap Ronnie Biggs (2005) by IWC Media/ Channel 4

Master Crime Museum – Great Train Robbery (2008) by Crime Network/ Brighter Picture/ Endemol

Mrs Biggs (2012) by ITV Studios

My Dad's a Villain (1999) Carlton TV

Once a Thief (1995) by Everyman/ BBC Television

Prisoner of Rio (1988) by Palace Pictures

Robbery (1967) by Paramount Pictures

Robberies of the Century (2001) Michael Hoff Productions, USA

Ronnie Biggs – The Last Escape (2005) by North One Television / Sky One

Ronnie Biggs – Secret Tapes Revealed (2011) Channel 5

Secret History – The Great Train Robbery (1999) by Blakeways/ Ten Alps/ Channel 4

The Great Paper Chase (1989) by BBC Television

The Great Train Robbery (1964) by World in Action/ ITV, Season 2 no 26

The Great Train Robbery (1978) by Man Alive/ BBC Television

The Great Train Robbery (2008) by Master Crime Museum

The Great Train Robbery (2012) by ITV Studios

The Great Train Robbery (2014) by Acorn Productions/ BBC

The Great Train Robbery's Missing Mastermind (2012) by Lion Production/ Channel 4

The Great Trainer Robbers' Secret Tapes Revealed (2011) by Crime Network/ Channel 5

The Legend of Ronnie Biggs (2002) by Meridian TV/ MMTV Production/ Channel 5

Underworld (1994) by BBC Television

Index